LEARN
JAPANESE
NIHONGO
THE FAST AND FUN WAY

SECOND EDITION

by Nobuo Akiyama
Professorial Lecturer, Japanese Language
The Paul H. Nitze School of
Advanced International Studies,
The Johns Hopkins University

Carol Akiyama
Language Training Consultant
Washington, D.C.

To help you pace your learning, we've included
stopwatches *like the one above* throughout
the book to mark each 15-minute interval.
You can read one of these units each day
or pace yourself according to your needs.

BARRON'S

CONTENTS

All inquiries should be addressed to:
Barron's Educational Series, Inc.
250 Wireless Boulevard
Hauppauge, New York 11788
http://www.barronseduc.com

International Standard Book No. 0-7641-0623-6

Library of Congress Catalog Card No. 98-73386

Cover and Book Design Milton Glaser, Inc.
Illustrations Juan Suarez

Maps © Copyright Japan National Tourist
Organization. Used with permission.

PRINTED IN THE UNITED STATES
OF AMERICA
98765432

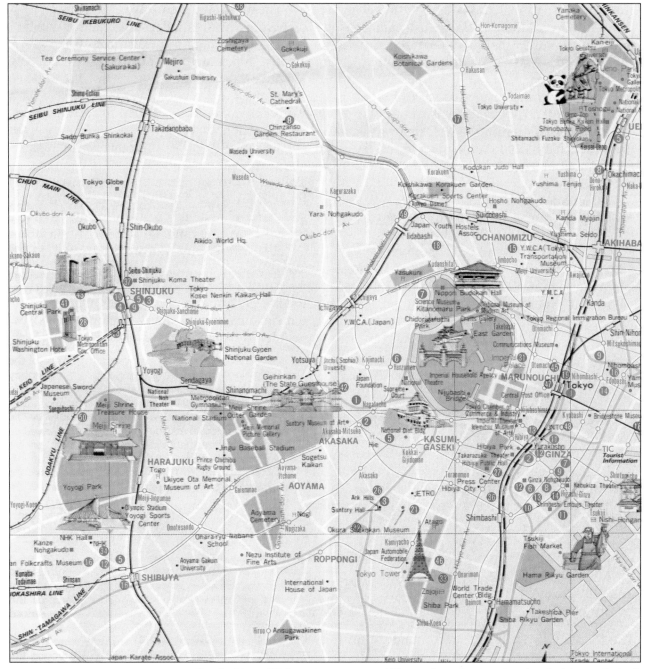

(*From* Tourist Map of Tokyo, *Japan National Tourist Organization. Reprinted with permission.*)

Studying Japanese will reward you with skills and insights you can use for many years to come. Whether your interest in Japan is business, pleasure, or both, you're about to enter a unique and exciting culture.

Japan has a large population, estimated at close to 130 million at the turn of the century.

The land area is about 144,000 square miles, or 372,000 square kilometers. That's about one twenty-fifth the size of the United States.

Japan's four main islands and roughly 3,000 smaller ones run in a general northeast-to-southwest direction. The length is about

1,860 miles, or 3,000 kilometers. Although many foreigners think of Japan as small—a few tiny islands in the Pacific off the east coast of Asia—it's larger in size than the United Kingdom, Germany, or Italy.

The temperature zones range from the subarctic to the subtropical. Hokkaido, far to the north, is cold and snowy. Okinawa, far to the south, is hot and humid. Tokyo, on the main island of Honshu, is the halfway point between these extremes of climate.

Japan has sights and attractions to please every taste. For visitors, it's a chance to see two different worlds: the great economic power with its skyscrapers, superhighways, advanced computer technology, high fashion, and avant-garde pop culture also has its wood-and-paper houses, streets too narrow for a car, handcrafted folkware, tea ceremony, Kabuki theater, and sumo wrestling.

The Japanese themselves are used to this dichotomy of the modern and the traditional in their everyday lives. Turn the corner of an elegant Ginza street in Tokyo, and find a tiny temple or shrine. Buy a ticket for the bullet train, and the clerk may verify your seat on a high-tech computer and then figure the price on a wooden abacus.

To make the most of your visit to Japan, above all, get out and explore. If you're in Tokyo, try to see more than just the tourist hotel areas. If you have time, visit Kyoto and other cities, and the countryside as well. In the cities, public transportation is excellent. Inter-city trains are frequent, fast, and efficient.

You've already taken an important step toward enjoying the fascinating, multi-dimensional culture that is Japan. You've decided to learn some Japanese!

JAPANESE PRONUNCIATION

Japanese isn't difficult to pronounce if you follow a few simple guidelines. Take the time to read this section, and try out each sound on the vowel and consonant charts.

To make it even easier for you, each time a new word is introduced in this book, the pronunciation is also shown.

We start with the vowels. If you have studied Spanish, it may help you to know that Japanese vowels are more like those of Spanish than English.

VOWELS

The following vowels are short and pure, with *no glide*—that is, they are not diphthongs.

Japanese Vowel	English Equivalent	Example
a	as in father	akai (*ah-kah-ee*) red
e	as in men	ebi (*eh-bee*) shrimp
i	as in see	imi (*ee-mee*) meaning
o	as in boat	otoko (*oh-toh-koh*) male
u	as in food	uma (*oo-mah*) horse

The following vowels are like the ones above, but they are held longer.

Japanese Vowel	English Equivalent	Example
ā	as in father, but lengthened	batā (*bah-tah*) butter
ei	as in men, but lengthened	eigo (*eh-goh*) English
ii	as in see, but lengthened	iiharu (*ee-hah-roo*) insist
ō	as in boat, but lengthened	ōsama (*oh-sah-mah*) king
ū	as in food, but lengthened	yūbin (*yoo-been*) mail

And keep in mind these points:
1. Long vowels are important; pronouncing a long vowel incorrectly can result in a different word or even an unintelligible one.
   For example, obasan (*oh-bah-sahn*) means aunt
                obāsan (*oh-bah-sahn*) means grandmother

                ojisan (*oh-jee-sahn*) means uncle
                ojiisan (*oh-jee-sahn*) means grandfather

                seki (*seh-kee*) means seat
                seiki (*seh-kee*) means century
2. Sometimes the **i** and the **u** aren't pronounced. This usually occurs between voiceless consonants (p, t, k, ch, f, h, s, sh), or at the end of a word following a voiceless consonant. Here's an example you may already know:
                sukiyaki (*skee-yah-kee*)
   This word for a popular Japanese dish begins with **skee,** not **soo.** The **u** is not pronounced. One more example:
                tabemashita (*tah-beh-mahsh-tah*) I ate
   The **i** is not pronounced.

CONSONANTS

With a few exceptions, Japanese consonants are similar to those of English. Note those that are different:

f   The English **f** is pronounced with a passage of air between the upper teeth and the lower lip. To make the Japanese **f**, blow air lightly between your lips as if you were just beginning a whistle.

g   Always as in **go**, never as in **age**. You may also hear it pronounced as the **ng** sound in si**ng**, but not at the beginning of a word.

r   This is different from the English **r**. To make the Japanese **r**, lightly touch the tip of your tongue to the bony ridge behind the upper teeth, almost in the English **d** position. It's more like the Spanish **r**, but it's not flapped or trilled.

s   Always hissed, as in **so**, never voiced, as in hi**s** or plea**s**ure.

And note the following points as well:

1. If you have trouble making these consonants the Japanese way, your English pronunciation will be intelligible and will not be considered incorrect.
2. Some Japanese consonants are doubled. In English, this is just a feature of spelling and often doesn't affect pronunciation. In Japanese, the doubling is important and may change the meaning of a word.

   For example:

       kite kudasai (*kee-teh koo-dah-sah-ee*) means
           "Please put it (clothing) on."
       kitte kudasai (*keet-teh koo-dah-sah-ee*) means
           "Please cut it."

   In a word with a doubled consonant, don't say the consonant twice—just hold the sound longer.

HOW ENGLISH AND JAPANESE ARE SIMILAR

If you know English, you may already know more Japanese than you think. Thousands of English "loan words" are in everyday use in Japan. Most of these common words have been borrowed with no change in meaning. *But the pronunciation has been changed.*

This can be tricky. On the one hand, you're secure with the familiarity of the words. On the other, if you pronounce them as you're used to doing, you won't be understood. And you probably won't understand the words when Japanese use them. What should you do? Try to pronounce them the Japanese way.

Here are some examples of familiar words with somewhat different pronunciations in Japanese:

English	Japanese	Pronunciation
gasoline	**gasorin**	*gah-soh-reen*
pocket	**poketto**	*poh-keht-toh*
pink	**pinku**	*peen-koo*
ballpoint pen	**bōru pen**	*boh-roo pehn*
supermarket	**sūpā**	*soo-pah*
word processor	**wāpuro**	*wah-poo-roh*
dress	**wanpīsu**	*wahn-pee-soo*

(If you didn't get that last one, think of "one piece"—as opposed to "two piece." Now it makes sense, doesn't it?)

HOW ENGLISH AND JAPANESE ARE DIFFERENT

The important differences between English and Japanese are the politeness requirements, sometimes called **levels of language**, or **politeness levels**.

The Japanese language reflects the importance of interpersonal relationships in the society. Other languages, of course, have ways of expressing degrees of formality in a relationship or situation. But the Japanese have more ways than most, and they take them very seriously.

Knowing the appropriate language for respect, courtesy, and relative social status in Japanese takes considerable time and study. It is, of course, beyond our scope here.

For the most part, this book teaches you an all-purpose level of language that you can use in many situations. Thus in some dialogues the language isn't exactly as the Japanese would speak it—the conversations between American tourist Mark Smith and his wife, Mary, for example. In real Japanese, a married couple would use a more informal level with each other and their children.

In dialogues with people in service industries, such as clerks in stores or flight attendants on airplanes, the characters *do* use the appropriate level of language—the extra-polite words and verb endings that their positions require.

These adjustments will help you get started.

Now begin. Just 15 minutes a day—that's all you need. It's fast, it's fun, and before you know it, you'll be communicating in Japanese!

GETTING TO KNOW PEOPLE

(hee-toh) (toh) (shee-REE-ah-oo)
Hito To Shiriau

	(hah-NAH-shee-mah-shoh)	
1	**Hanashimashō**	
	Let's Talk	

When you arrive in Japan, you'll need to know some basic expressions. The easy dialogues below will enable you to ask for help, to greet people, and to have brief conversations.

Read each dialogue aloud several times. The words in parentheses will help you pronounce the Japanese correctly.

Mark Smith, his wife, Mary, their son, Paul, and their daughter, Anne, have just arrived at Narita Airport, about 60 kilometers from downtown Tokyo. They've claimed their luggage and passed through customs. Now they want to find the bus for Tokyo. They approach a porter.

	(CHOHT-toh) *(soo-mee-mah-sehn)* *(gah)*	
MARK	**Chotto, sumimasen ga . . .**	Excuse me . . .
	(HAH-ee) *(nahn)(deh-shoh)*	
PORTER	**Hai, nan deshō.**	Yes, may I help you?
	(toh-kyoh) *(yoo-kee)* *(noh)* *(BAH-soo)*	
MARK	**Tokyo yuki no basu no**	Where do we get the bus for Tokyo?
	(noh-ree-bah) *(wah)* *(doh-koh)* *(dehs)* *(KAH)*	
	noriba wa, doko desu ka.	
	(ah-soh-koh) *(dehs)*	
PORTER	**Asoko desu.**	It's right over there.
	(DOH-moh) *(ah-ree-gah-toh)*	
MARK	**Dōmo arigatō.**	Thank you.

While riding the bus to Tokyo, Mark strikes up a conversation with Koji Nishida, a Japanese man sitting next to him.

(kohn-nee-chee-wah)
MARK **Konnichiwa.**

Good afternoon.

MR. NISHIDA **Konnichiwa.**

Good afternoon.

(wah-tahk-shee)   *(nah-mah-eh)*
MARK **Watakushi no   namae wa,**

My name is Mark Smith.

(MAH-koo SOO-mee-soo)   *(ah-nah-tah)*
Māku Sumisu desu.   Anata

What's your name?

(oh-nah-mah-eh)
no onamae wa.

(NEE-shee-dah) (KOH-jee)
MR. NISHIDA **Nishida   Kōji desu.**

I'm Koji Nishida. Glad to meet you, Mr. Smith.

(hah-JEE-meh-mahsh-teh)   *(sahn)*
Hajimemashite, Sumisu san.

MARK **Hajimemashite.**

Glad to meet *you.*

(DOH-koh) (kah-rah)
MR. NISHIDA **Doko   kara**

Where are you from?

(ee-rahsh-shah-ee-mahsh-tah)
irrasshaimashita ka.

(nyoo-yoh-koo)   (kee-mahsh-tah)
MARK **Nyūyōku kara kimashita.**

I'm from New York.

(nee-hohn)   (hah-JEE-meh-teh)
MR. NISHIDA **Nihon wa, hajimete**

Is this your first time in Japan?

desu ka.

(koh-reh)
MARK **Hai. Kore ga, watakushi**

Yes. This is my family—my wife, my son, and

(KAH-zoh-koo)   (TSOO-mah toh)
no kazoku desu. Tsuma to,

my daughter.

(moos-koh)   (moo-soo-meh)
musuko to, musume desu.

MR. NISHIDA **Hajimemashite.**

Glad to meet you.

About two hours later, the bus arrives at the terminal in Tokyo. As they leave the bus, Mr. Nishida helps the Smiths with their luggage, and then they say goodbye.

(tskee-mahsh-tah)   (yoh)
MR. NISHIDA **Tsukimashita yo.**

Here we are. Let me help you carry your

(soo-tsoo keh-soo)   (oh) (hah-koh-boo)
Sūtsu kēsu   o hakobu,

suitcases.

(oh-TEH-tsoo-dah-ee)   (shee-mah-shoh)
otetsudai o   shimashō.

	(goh-zah-ee-mahs)	
MARK	**Arigatō gozaimasu.**	Thank you . . .
	(ēē-eh) (dōh) (ee-tah-shee-mahsh-teh)	
MR. NISHIDA	**Iie, dō itashimashite.**	You're welcome.
	(sah-YŌH-nah-rah)	
MARK	**Sayōnara.**	Goodbye.
MR. NISHIDA	**Sayōnara.**	Goodbye.

Match the English expressions with their Japanese equivalents. Look back at the dialogues if you need to.

1. Konnichiwa.

2. Watakushi no namae wa, _____ desu.

3. Sayōnara.

4. Iie, dō itashimashite.

5. Arigatō gozaimasu.

6. Chotto, sumimasen ga.

7. Hajimemashite.

8. Kore ga, watakushi no kazoku desu.

9. Anata no onamae wa.

10. Hai.

a. Excuse me.

b. Yes.

c. Good afternoon.

d. My name is . . .

e. What's your name?

f. This is my family.

g. Glad to meet you.

h. Thank you.

i. You're welcome.

j. Goodbye.

HITO TO MONO
(moh-noh)

People and Things

When speaking Japanese, one of the first things you need to know is how to use nouns—people and things. Let's talk about *things* first. It's easier in Japanese than in English. Why? You don't have to worry about singular and plural. You don't have to worry about articles.

Look at these examples:

(hohn)
hon
a book

(moht-teh) *(ee-mahs)*
Hon o motte   imasu.
I have a book.

hon
some books

Hon o motte imasu.
I have some books.

Here are a few more. Write the nouns in the blanks:

(oo-chee)
uchi
house, houses

1. _____

(sheen-boon)
shinbun
newspaper, newspapers

2. _____

(kee)
ki
tree, trees

3. _____

(ah-shee)
ashi
foot, feet

4. _____

ANSWERS

Nouns 1. uchi 2. shinbun 3. ki 4. ashi

9

For *people*, it's different, but still easy. In most cases, to form the plural you add the suffix **-tachi**. Look at these examples of singular and plural nouns:

(koh-doh-moh)
kodomo
child

(tah-chee)
kodomo tachi
children

(oh-toh-koh) (koh)
otoko no ko
boy

otoko no ko tachi
boys

(ohn-nah)
onna no ko
girl

onna no ko tachi
girls

(hah-hah) (oh-yah)
haha   oya
mother

haha oya tachi
mothers

Write the nouns in the blanks below. Look back at the examples when you need help.

1. child _____

2. boy _____

3. girl _____

4. mother _____

5. children _____

6. boys _____

7. girls _____

8. mothers _____

Now test your knowledge of singular and plural by writing the Japanese for these people and things.

a. boy _____

b. trees _____

c. girls _____

d. children _____

e. child _____

f. mothers _____

g. foot _____

h. newspapers _____

i. house _____

j. tree _____

(AH-ee-sah-tsoo)
AISATSU TO NAMAE
Greetings and Names

As you read the dialogues earlier in this lesson you may have noticed that the English word "Hello" wasn't used. That's because Japanese has no equivalent word. Instead, greetings are based on the time of day: "Good morning," "Good afternoon," and "Good evening." You should learn these expressions:

(oh-hah-yoh)	(goh-zah-ee-mahs)	
Ohayō	**gozaimasu.**	Good morning.
Konnichiwa.		Good afternoon.
(kohn-bahn-wah)		
Konbanwa.		Good evening.

How would you greet someone at 9 A.M.?   1. _____

at 7 P.M.?   2. _____

at 2 P.M.?   3. _____

11

In English, these greetings are often followed by the phrases, "How are you?" and "Fine, thanks." Japanese don't use this exchange with people they see daily. They use the equivalent expression only when they have not seen someone in a while, only with adults, and only in formal situations. They don't use it when meeting someone for the first time.

Look at this exchange and pronounce the words. There will be times when you'll need this!

(oh-GEHN-kee)
Ogenki desu ka.   How are you? (Literally, "Are you well?")
    (oh-KAH-geh-sah-mah)(deh)
Hai, okagesama   **de.**   Fine, thanks. (Literally, "I'm well because of you.")

Names are used differently in Japanese than in English. The differences are important, and the following guidelines will help you:

Japanese use family names first, first names last.
Nishida Koji is Mr. Nishida. Koji is his first name. When Japanese introduce themselves to each other, they say the family name first. However, they know that English speakers do it the opposite way.

Japanese prefer family names, not first names.
Japanese adults rarely use first names. Even among close friends, family names are the rule, first names the exception. Unless a Japanese specifically asks you to use his or her first name, you should use the family name.

Japanese use titles with names.
When speaking to someone or when referring to another person, Japanese use **san** after the family name. It's like the English Mr., Mrs., Ms., or Miss. Even when using a friend's first name, you should add **san**. For example, Mark Smith would say "Koji san," not "Koji," if he were using Nishida san's first name. Remember, you *never* use **san** when speaking of yourself.

With names of **children**, it's a little different. Japanese use young children's first names
(chahn)
followed by **chan**, older children's first names followed by **san**. Mr. Nishida's 5-year-old son,
(goh-roh)
Goro, is called Goro chan. When Goro gets older, he'll be called Goro san.

One evening several weeks after their bus ride from the airport, Mark Smith and Koji Nishida run into each other in the lobby of Mark's hotel in Tokyo. They have a brief conversation. Can you fill in the blanks with the equivalent Japanese expressions?

MARK   **Good evening, Mr. Nishida.**   1. _____

MR. NISHIDA   **Good evening, Mr. Smith.**   2. _____

MARK   **How are you?**   3. _____

MR. NISHIDA   **Fine, thanks.**   4. _____

KAZOKU NI TSUITE HANASHIMASHŌ
(tsoo-ee-teh)
Let's Talk about the Family

In English, when you talk to or about a member of your family, the word you use is the same. For example, if you're talking to your mother, you can call her "Mother." If you're talking about her to someone outside the family, you still use the word "mother."

In Japanese, it's different. There are two sets of words to describe family members. One is used only when talking to members of your own family or when talking about members of someone else's family. The other is used only when talking about members of your own family to someone outside the family.

Does this sound complicated? The two charts that follow will make it much easier! Just look them over and refer to them whenever you need them.

(tah-NAH-kah keh)

TANAKA KE

The Tanaka Family

Jiro Tanaka is a Japanese boy. Here are the members of his family. He's telling Mark Smith about them. **You should use these words when talking to other people about your own family.**

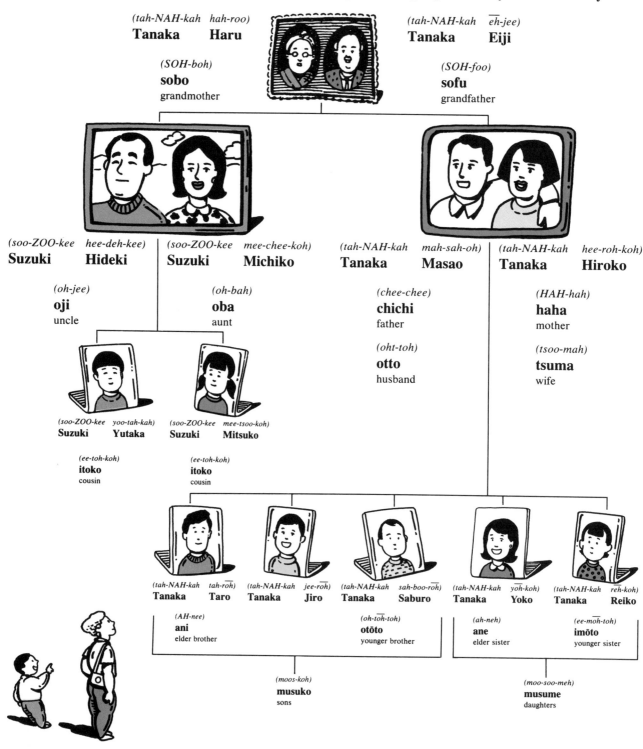

(tah-NAH-kah hah-roo)
Tanaka   Haru

(SOH-boh)
sobo
grandmother

(tah-NAH-kah eh-jee)
Tanaka   Eiji

(SOH-foo)
sofu
grandfather

(soo-ZOO-kee hee-deh-kee)
Suzuki   Hideki

(oh-jee)
oji
uncle

(soo-ZOO-kee mee-chee-koh)
Suzuki   Michiko

(oh-bah)
oba
aunt

(tah-NAH-kah mah-sah-oh)
Tanaka   Masao

(chee-chee)
chichi
father

(oht-toh)
otto
husband

(tah-NAH-kah hee-roh-koh)
Tanaka   Hiroko

(HAH-hah)
haha
mother

(tsoo-mah)
tsuma
wife

(soo-ZOO-kee yoo-tah-kah)
Suzuki   Yutaka

(ee-toh-koh)
itoko
cousin

(soo-ZOO-kee mee-tsoo-koh)
Suzuki   Mitsuko

(ee-toh-koh)
itoko
cousin

(tah-NAH-kah tah-roh)
Tanaka   Taro

(AH-nee)
ani
elder brother

(tah-NAH-kah jee-roh)
Tanaka   Jiro

(tah-NAH-kah sah-boo-roh)
Tanaka   Saburo

(oh-toh-toh)
otōto
younger brother

(tah-NAH-kah yoh-koh)
Tanaka   Yoko

(ah-neh)
ane
elder sister

(tah-NAH-kah reh-koh)
Tanaka   Reiko

(ee-moh-toh)
imōto
younger sister

(moos-koh)
musuko
sons

(moo-soo-meh)
musume
daughters

Tanaka Jiro   Mark Smith

14

Here is Jiro Tanaka's family again. This time, Mark Smith is talking to him and another friend about the members of the family. **You should use these words when talking to other people about members of their family or someone else's family, or to members of your own family.**

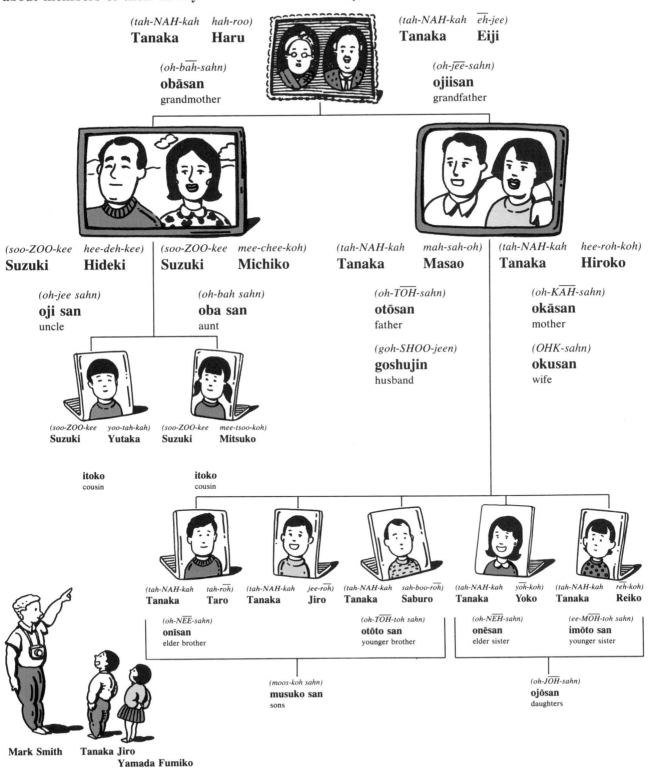

(tah-NAH-kah   hah-roo)
Tanaka   Haru

(oh-bah-sahn)
obāsan
grandmother

(tah-NAH-kah   eh-jee)
Tanaka   Eiji

(oh-jee-sahn)
ojiisan
grandfather

(soo-ZOO-kee   hee-deh-kee)
Suzuki   Hideki

(oh-jee sahn)
oji san
uncle

(soo-ZOO-kee   mee-chee-koh)
Suzuki   Michiko

(oh-bah sahn)
oba san
aunt

(tah-NAH-kah   mah-sah-oh)
Tanaka   Masao

(oh-TOH-sahn)
otōsan
father

(goh-SHOO-jeen)
goshujin
husband

(tah-NAH-kah   hee-roh-koh)
Tanaka   Hiroko

(oh-KAH-sahn)
okāsan
mother

(OHK-sahn)
okusan
wife

(soo-ZOO-kee   yoo-tah-kah)
Suzuki   Yutaka

(soo-ZOO-kee   mee-tsoo-koh)
Suzuki   Mitsuko

itoko
cousin

itoko
cousin

(tah-NAH-kah   tah-roh)
Tanaka   Taro

(oh-NEE-sahn)
onīsan
elder brother

(tah-NAH-kah   jee-roh)
Tanaka   Jiro

(tah-NAH-kah   sah-boo-roh)
Tanaka   Saburo

(oh-TOH-toh sahn)
otōto san
younger brother

(tah-NAH-kah   yoh-koh)
Tanaka   Yoko

(oh-NEH-sahn)
onēsan
elder sister

(tah-NAH-kah   reh-koh)
Tanaka   Reiko

(ee-MOH-toh sahn)
imōto san
younger sister

(moos-koh sahn)
musuko san
sons

(oh-JOH-sahn)
ojōsan
daughters

Mark Smith   **Tanaka Jiro**
Yamada Fumiko

15

Let's see how easy it is to talk about the family! Fill in the missing words.

1. My *wife*   Watakushi no _____

2. Your *aunt*   Anata no _____

3. Mr. Suzuki's *son*   Suzuki san no _____

4. My *grandfather*   Watakushi no _____

5. Your elder *sister*   Anata no _____

6. Jiro's *mother*   Jiro san no _____

7. My *son*   Watakushi no _____

8. Your *daughters*   Anata no _____

9. Mr. Nishida's *uncle*   Nishida san no _____

10. Our *father*   Watakushi tachi no _____

Now that you know the members of the family, you'll want to see where they live. On the next page is Jiro Tanaka's house. It has both western-style and Japanese-style rooms. Most Japanese homes have at least one "**tatami** room," with woven mats on the floor. It's an all-purpose room: a sitting room by day, it becomes a bedroom at night when the **futon**, or mattresses are spread on the floor and made up for sleeping. In most homes the bathroom area has separate rooms for the tub, sink, and toilet.

Look at Jiro's house and practice saying the Japanese words.

UCHI
A House

(oh-TEH-ah-rah-ee)
otearai
toilet

(reh-zoh-koh) *(toh)* *(sehn-mehn)* *(dah-ee)*
reizōko **to** **senmen** **dai**
refrigerator door sink

(dah-ee-doh-koh-roh)
daidokoro
kitchen

(gah-soo-rehn-jee) *(gehn-kahn)*
gasu renji **genkan**
stove entry for removing shoes

(yohk-soh)
yokusō
bathtub

(nah-gah-shee)
nagashi
kitchen sink

(oh-SHEE-ee-reh)
oshiire
closet

(ee-MAH)
ima
living room

(shoh-jee)
shōji
sliding wooden and paper
screen

(ee-soo)
isu
chair

(tah-tah-mee)
tatami
woven mat floor

(teh-boo-roo)
tēburu
table

(foo-tohn)
futon
bedding on the floor

(soh-fah)
sofā
sofa

(sheen-shee-tsoo)
shinshitsu
bedroom

(roh-kah)
rōka
hallway

(mah-doh)
mado
window

(nee-wah)
niwa
garden

(kah-ee-dahn)
kaidan
stairway

ARRIVAL

(tōh-chah-koo)
Tōchaku

	(hoh-teh-roo)	*(deh)*
2	**Hoteru de**	
	At the hotel	

You'll probably book your hotel room from home—at least for your first night in Japan. But whether you have a reservation or not, you'll want to know some basic words that describe the services and facilities you expect to find at your hotel. Learn these words first, and notice how they are used in the dialogue you will read later.

hoteru
hotel

(yoh-yah-koo)
yoyaku
reservation

(neh-dahn)
nedan
price

(heh-yah)
heya
room

(bah-soo-ROO-moo)
basurūmu
bathroom

(pah-soo-pōh-toh)
pasupōto
passport

(kah-kah-ree-een)
hoteru no kakariin
hotel clerk

(doh-ah)
doa
door

mado
window

(mēh-doh)
mēdo
maid

(nah-gah-meh)
nagame
view

18

(dah-ee-meh-shee)
Daimeishi
Pronouns

Now let's learn some pronouns in Japanese:

watakushi I

anata ....you

(kah-reh)
kare ....he

(kah-noh-joh)
kanojo ....she

(wah-tahk-shee-tah-chee)
watakushitachi ....we

(ah-nah-tah-tah-chee)
anatatachi ....you (plural)

(kah-reh-rah)
karera ....they (males; males *and* females)

(kah-noh-joh-tah-chee)
kanojotachi ....they (females)

In Japanese, the use of "that person" for "he" or "she" is quite common. Although, strictly speaking, this isn't a pronoun, it's helpful to think of it as such.

(ah-noh hee-toh)
ano   hito ....he, she (that person)

(ah-noh hee-toh-tah-chee)
ano   hitotachi ....they (those persons)

The following pronouns may be used for both *singular* and *plural*:

kore ....it, this
(soh-reh)
sore ....that
(ah-reh)
are ....that (over there)

19

As you learn to speak more Japanese, you'll notice an interesting difference about the way the Japanese use *personal pronouns* (I, you, he, she, we, they): If the meaning is clear from the context, the Japanese usually prefer to omit the personal pronoun.

If two people are talking, the exchange might go like this:

	(eh)(ee-kee-mahs)	
MARK	**Doko e ikimasu ka.**	Where are you going?
	(KYOH-toh)	
MR. TANAKA	**Kyoto e ikimasu.**	I'm going to Kyoto.

The English sentences contain the personal pronouns "I" and "you." But if you check with the above pronoun chart, you'll see that the Japanese sentences don't use the equivalent words, "**anata**" and "**watakushi**." In this exchange, the meaning is clear without the pronouns, so they're dropped.

Now let's practice. In the following sentences, fill in the missing words:

1. _____(I)_____ wa, _____(passport)_____ o, motte imasu.

   a. _____ b. _____

2. _____(he)_____ ga, _____(hotel)_____ ni imasu.

   a. _____ b. _____

Now for some more adventures of Mark Smith and his family as they arrive at their hotel in Tokyo. Read each line of the dialogue out loud to practice your pronunciation.

	(ee-RAHS-shah-ee-mah-seh)	
CLERK	**Konnichiwa. Irrashaimase.**	Good afternoon. Welcome.
	(foo-tah)	
MARK	**Konnichiwa. Futa heya**	Good afternoon. We have a reservation for
	(shee-teh) (ah-ree-mahs)	
	yoyaku ga shite arimasu.	two rooms.
	Watakushi no namae wa, Māku	My name is Mark Smith.
	Sumisu desu.	

ANSWERS

Fill in 1. a. Watakushi b. pasupōto 2. a. Kare b. hoteru

20

CLERK   **Hai, arimasu, Sumisu san.**   Yes, Mr. Smith, we have your reservation. Would

(koh-noh) (yōh-shee) (kah-kee-kohn-deh)
Kono yōshi ni kakikonde   you fill out this form, please?

(koo-dah-sah-ee)
kudasai.

        (moh-CHEE-rohn)
MARK   **Hai, mochiron.**   Yes, of course.

           (mee-seh-teh)
CLERK   **Pasupōto o misete**   May I have your passport, please?

(ee-tah-dah-keh-mah-sehn)
itadakemasen ka.

        (dōh-zoh)
MARK   **Hai, dōzo.**   Here you are.

      (NAHN) (nee-chee) (oh-toh-mah-ree)
CLERK   **Nan nichi   otomari desu ka.**   How long will you be staying with us?

(yah-koo) (ees-shōō-kahn) (toh-mah-ree-mahs)
MARK   **Yaku   isshūkan   tomarimasu.**   About a week.

(wah-kah-ree-mahsh-tah)
CLERK   **Wakarimashita.**   I see.

(shoo-KOO-hah-koo) (dah-ee) (nee)
MARK   **Shukuhaku   dai   ni**   Is breakfast included in the price of the room?

(chōh-shoh-koo) (foo-KOO-mah-reh-teh)
chōshoku wa fukumarete

(ee-mahs)
imasu ka.

      (ēē-eh)   (ee-mah-sehn)
CLERK   **Iie, fukumarete imasen.**   No, it isn't. But we have a nice coffee shop.

(keh-reh-doh-moh) (koh-koh) (ēē)(koh-hēē)
Keredomo   koko ni ii kōhī

(shohp-poo) (goh-zah-ee-mahs)
shoppu ga gozaimasu.

MARK   **Wakarimashita.**   I see.

(oh-heh-yah)   (jōō-rohk-kah-ee) (deh)
CLERK   **Oheya wa,   jūrokkai   de**   Your rooms are on the sixteenth floor.

gozaimasu.

MARK   **Nagame wa, ii desu ka.**   Is the view good?

        (toh-teh-moh)
CLERK   **Hai, totemo ii nagame desu.**   Yes, very good. Here are your keys.

(kah-gee)
Kore ga, oheya no kagi desu.

MARK **Arigatō. Erebētā wa doko**
(eh-reh-beh-tah)

desu ka.

Thank you. Where's the elevator?

CLERK **Asoko no migi gawa desu.**
(mee-gee) (gah-wah)

Gotaizai o, otanoshimi
(goh-TAH-ee-zah-ee) (oh-TAH-noh-shee-mee)

kudasai.

Over there on the right. Enjoy your stay with us.

Match these Japanese expressions with their English equivalents. Look back at the dialogue if you need to.

1. Wakarimashita.

2. Futa heya yoyaku ga shite arimasu.

3. Erebētā wa doko desu ka.

4. Nagame wa, ii desu ka.

5. Pasupōto o misete itadakemasen ka.

6. Hai, dōzo.

7. Konnichiwa.

8. Hai, mochiron.

a. Here you are.

b. May I have your passport, please?

c. Yes, of course.

d. Good afternoon.

e. Is the view good?

f. Where's the elevator?

g. We have a reservation for two rooms.

h. I see.

MOSHI SHITSUMON O SHITAI NARA
(moh-shee) (shee-tsoo-mohn) (shee-tah-ee) (nah-rah)
If You Want to Ask a Question

When you're traveling, you'll need to ask a lot of questions. For questions that can be answered with *yes* or *no*, it's easy. Just put the particle **ka** at the end of the sentence. The **ka** is almost like a question mark. You can think of it that way. And just raise your voice toward the end of the sentence the way you do in English.

Nagame wa ii desu. view good is	The view is good.
Nagame wa ii desu ka.	Is the view good?
Are wa Sumisu san desu. That Mr. Smith is	That's Mr. Smith.
Are wa Sumisu san desu ka.	Is that Mr. Smith?

ANSWERS

For other types of questions, become familiar with these key words.

(dah-reh)	
dare _____	WHO
(nah-nee)	
nan, nani _____	WHAT
doko _____	WHERE
(nahn-deh)	
nande _____	HOW
(nah-zeh)	
naze _____	WHY
(ee-tsoo)	
itsu _____	WHEN
(doh-reh) (doh-noh)	
dore, dono _____	WHICH

Now match up each question in the left column with its answer in the right column.

(yōh-koh)   (tah-beh-teh)

1. Yōko san wa, nani o tabete imasu ka.
                 eating

(tskee-mahs)

2. Kare wa, itsu tsukimasu ka.
                 arrives

3. Kare wa, doko ni tsukimasu ka.
   (ahn)

4. An san wa, Nihongo o hanashimasu ka.
   Japanese   speaks

(skee)

5. Anata wa, gohan ga suki desu ka.
                 like

(kōo-koh)

a. Kare wa kūkō ni tsukimasu.
   airport

(nee-hohn-goh) (hah-nah-shee-mahs)

b. Hai, Nihongo o hanashimasu.

(goh-hahn)

c. Gohan o tabete imasu.
   rice

(ah-shee-tah)

d. Ashita tsukimasu.
   tomorrow

e. Hai, gohan ga suki desu.

The phrase "there is" is useful to know in Japanese. It's the same in the singular and the plural, but it's different for people and things.

THERE IS, THERE ARE		
AFFIRMATIVE		NEGATIVE
IMASU	(People)	**IMASEN**
Mēdo ga imasu. There is a maid. There are maids.		**Mēdo ga imasen.** There's no maid. There are no maids.
ARIMASU	(Things)	**ARIMASEN**
Heya ga arimasu. There is a room. There are rooms.		**Heya ga arimasen.** There's no room. There are no rooms.

Can you fill in the blanks in this exercise?

1. Sumisu san ga _____ ka.   Hai, imasu.

2. _____ ga imasu ka.   Tanaka san ga imasu.

3. Nagame ga, ii desu _____ .   Hai, ii desu.

4. Basurūmu ga _____ ka.   Hai, arimasu.

5. Erebētā wa _____ desu _____ .   Asoko no migi gawa desu.

(doh-shee)

Dōshi
Verbs

It's difficult to get along without verbs—the words that express action. They're the only words in the sentence that can *do* anything. You'll want to learn some verbs and the different forms they take in Japanese.

You've already seen the first one—in the dialogues and elsewhere. It's the one that's equivalent to the English "am, is, are," the verb "to be."

(dah) **DA** to be		
	AFFIRMATIVE	NEGATIVE
PRESENT	**desu** I am, you are, he/she/it/ is, they are	(deh-wah) **dewa arimasen**
PAST	(dehsh-tah) **deshita** I was, you were, he/she/it was, they were	**dewa arimasen deshita**

Some important things about Japanese verbs:

They come at the end of the sentence.

They stay the same no matter what the subject is.

To form the negative:
(mahs)   (mah-sehn) PRESENT: change **-masu** to **-masen**
(mahsh-tah) (mah-sehn) (dehsh-tah) PAST: change **-mashita** to **-masen   deshita**

Now you're ready for some more verbs!

HANASU to speak	
AFFIRMATIVE	NEGATIVE
PRESENT	(hah-nah-shee-mahs) **hanashimasu** speak	(hah-nah-shee-mah-sehn) **hanashimasen** don't speak
PAST	(hah-nah-shee-mahsh-tah) **hanashimashita** spoke	(dehsh-tah) **hanashimasen deshita** didn't speak

Doesn't that look simple? The same word for *I speak, you speak, he speaks, we speak, they speak*! You can even use the present tense verb for future tense meanings. Although you won't be using it much in this book, the past tense is included here for your convenience.

We don't mean to imply that the Japanese verb system isn't complex—it is. There are different verb forms to use in different situations, depending on the courtesy level required. But our goal is to help you attain some basic conversational Japanese quickly. The verbs you're learning here use a safe, all-purpose degree of politeness. Later you will probably want to expand your knowledge of Japanese to learn the verb forms that express different levels of politeness.

(tskoo) **TSUKU** to arrive	
AFFIRMATIVE	**NEGATIVE**
PRESENT **tsukimasu** arrive	**tsukimasen** don't arrive
PAST **tsukimashita** arrived	**tsukimasen deshita** didn't arrive

(oo-tah-oo) **UTAU** to sing	
AFFIRMATIVE	**NEGATIVE**
PRESENT **utaimasu** sing	**utaimasen** don't sing
PAST **utaimashita** sang	**utaimasen deshita** didn't sing

Let's try an exercise to check your understanding thus far. Fill in the blanks with the Japanese.

(nee-hohn-jeen)
1. Yōko san wa, Nihonjin _____ ka.
   a Japanese   is

(zehn-zehn)
2. Watakushi wa, zen zen _____ .
   at all   don't sing

(kyoh)
3. Sumisu san ga, kyō kūkō ni _____ .
   today   arrives

4. Tanaka san wa, hoteru ni itsu _____ ka.
   will arrive

5. Kodomotachi wa, doko _____ ka?
   are

26

(joh-shee)
JOSHI
Particles

Japanese contains many particles—short words which are often called *post*positions because they come *after* other words. These particles help to identify the relationship of the word they follow to other important parts of the sentence.

You already know one particle—**ka**—which is used to form a question. Here's a list of the most commonly used particles:

wa/ga	Subject markers (more accurately, they occur with words that translate the English subject).
o	Direct object marker. (Sometimes, for emphasis, **ga** has this function).
ka	Question marker
no	Possessive marker
ni	Indirect object marker. Also translates English *to* (or *in* or *at* when it indicates where something is located).
e	Translates English *to* (in that direction, toward).
de	Translates English *at* when it indicates where an action takes place. Also *by* (by bus) and *of* (made of wood).

You've seen these words in the lessons so far, and you've probably been wondering about them. Now you know what they are!

Study and repeat aloud these parts of a hotel room.

(hoh-teh-roo noh heh-yah)
Hoteru   no heya
A Hotel Room

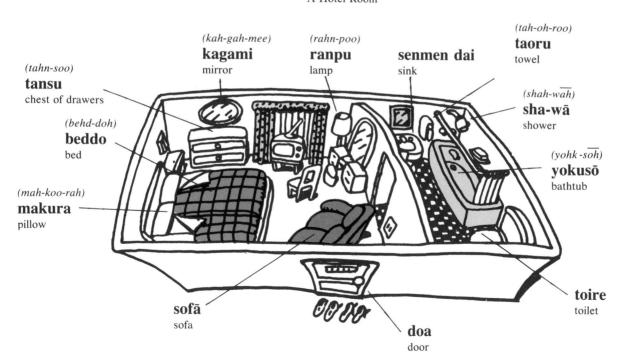

(tahn-soo)
tansu
chest of drawers

(behd-doh)
beddo
bed

(mah-koo-rah)
makura
pillow

(kah-gah-mee)
kagami
mirror

(rahn-poo)
ranpu
lamp

senmen dai
sink

(tah-oh-roo)
taoru
towel

(shah-wah)
sha-wā
shower

(yohk-soh)
yokusō
bathtub

sofā
sofa

doa
door

toire
toilet

27

Can you read the following story aloud and understand what it means? Read it several times and then answer the questions below.

Māku Sumisu san wa, kazoku to Tokyo no hoteru ni imasu.

Heya wa, jūrokkai ni arimasu. Nagame wa, ii desu. Hoteru

niwa, ii kōhī shoppu ga arimasu. Sumisu san to kazoku wa,

(tah-beh-mahs)

chōshoku o kōhī shoppu de tabemasu.

Answer true or false.

1. Māku Sumisu san wa, kazoku to uchi ni imasu.   1. _____

2. Sumisu san wa, kazoku to hoteru ni imasu.   2. _____

3. Nagame wa, ii desu.   3. _____

4. Hoteru niwa, kōhī shoppu ga arimasen.   4. _____

5. Sumisu san to kazoku wa, chōshoku o kōhī shoppu de tabemasen.   5. _____

SEEING THE SIGHTS

(kahn-kōh   kehn-boo-tsoo)
Kankō Kenbutsu

3	*(ah-roo-ee-teh)* *(mee-chee)* *(sah-gah-soo)* ## Aruite michi o sagasu Finding Your Way on Foot

"How do I get to . . . ?" "Where is the nearest subway?" "Is the museum straight ahead?" You'll be asking directions wherever you travel. Acquaint yourself with these words and phrases that will make getting around easier. Don't forget to read each line aloud several times to practice your pronunciation. Act out each part to be certain you understand the new words.

(Paul and Anne Smith set out on their first day to visit a museum.)

(bee-joo-tsoo-kahn)
ANNE **Bijutsukan ga doko ni aru**
(keh-kahn)   *(kee-kee-mah-shōh)*
ka, keikan ni kikimashō.
policeman

Let's ask the policeman where the museum is.

PAUL **Chotto sumimasen ga,**
(nee-wah) *(dōh)* *(eet-tah-rah)*
bijutsukan niwa   dō ittara ii
(oh-shee-eh-teh)
ka, oshiete kudasai.

Excuse me, sir, can you tell us how to get to the museum?

(kah-dōh)
POLICEMAN **Ii desu yo. Kado**

(mah-deh) *(mahs-soo-goo)* *(eet-teh)*
made   massugu   itte, migi ni

(mah-gaht-teh)
magatte kudasai. Sore kara
Then
(tsoo-gee) *(kōh-sah-tehn)*
tsugi no kōsaten made itte,

(hee-dah-ree)
hidari ni magatte kudasai.

Certainly. Go straight ahead to the corner and turn right. Then go to the next intersection and turn left. Continue to the first traffic light. The museum is there, inside a small park.

(sohsh-teh) (sah-ee-shoh) (sheen-gōh)
Soshite   saisho no shingō
and

(ee-kee-mahs)
made ikimasu. Bijutsukan

(soh-koh) (chēe-sah-ee)(kōh-ehn)
wa, soko no chiisai   kōen no

(nah-kah)
naka ni arimasu.

(goh-zah-ee-mahsh-tah)
PAUL   Dōmo arigatō gozaimashita.   Many thanks.

(dōh ee-tah-shee-mahsh-teh)
POLICEMAN   Dō itashimashite.   You're welcome.

(after having followed the directions)

(bee-roo)
ANNE   Kono biru wa, bijutsukan   This building is not the museum. It's the post
        building
                                          office.
dewa arimasen. Sore wa,

(yōo-been   kyoh-koo)
yūbin   kyoku desu.

(toh-nee-kah-koo) (mōh) (oh-soh-ee) (kah-rah)
PAUL   Tonikaku   mō   osoi   kara,   Anyway, since it's already late, let's go back to
(moh-doh-ree-mah-shōh)
hoteru ni modorimashō.   the hotel.

Can you answer these true-false questions based on the dialogue?

1. Pōru san wa, keikan ni yūbin kyoku ga doko ni aru ka, kikimasu.   1. _____
                                                    asks

2. Keikan wa, kare ni, kado made massugu itte, migi ni   2. _____
      (oh-shee-eh-mahs)
   magaru yō oshiemasu.

3. Bijutsukan wa, chiisai kōen no naka ni arimasu.   3. _____

4. Kono biru wa, bijutsukan dewa arimasen.   4. _____

5. Sore wa, hoteru desu.   5. _____

ANSWERS

True-false 1. False 2. True 3. True 4. True 5. False

30

Yaku ni tatsu chiisai kotoba

(yah-koo   nee   tah-tsoo)   (chēē-sah-ee)   (koh-toh-bah)

Helpful little words

(ah-meh-ree-kah)

Merī san wa, Amerika   ni imasu.
Mary   in

(yoh-koo) (nyōō-yōh-koo)

Kono hito wa, yoku   Nyūyōku e   ikimasu.
            often   to goes

(mah-ee-nee-chee) (pahn-yah)

Jirō san wa, mainichi   panya e ikimasu.
every day   bakery   to

(pahn)   (kaht-teh)

Jirō san wa, panya de pan o katte imasu.
           at   bread   is buying

Tanaka san wa, Nihon kara kimashita.
              from   comes

(gahk-kōh)

Kono otoko no ko wa, gakkō   ni imasu.
               school   at

Jirō san wa, mainichi gakkō e ikimasu.
                    to

In English, these words are prepositions—they come before the word or words they modify, that is, a noun or noun phrase.

to Tokyo   from the United States

at school   in the post office

In Japanese, they're postpositions—they come after the word or words they modify. And, as you have learned already, they're called **particles.**

Tokyo e   **Amerika kara**

gakko de   **yūbin kyoku ni**

Can you fill in the correct particle?

1. Pōru san wa, Nyūyōku _____ imasu.
     in

2. Tanaka san wa, Nihon _____ kimashita.
     from

3. Kono otoko no ko wa, gakkō _____ imasu.
     at

4. Kono hito wa, mainichi yūbin kyoku _____ ikimasu.
     to

5. Keikan ga, kado _____ imasu.
     at

Now match up the following:

1. at the corner	a. kūkō e
2. to the airport	b. gakkō ni
3. at school	c. panya de
4. from Japan	d. kado ni
5. at the bakery	e. Nihon kara

Imi ga takusan aru kotoba o mō sukoshi

(ee-mee) *(tahk-sahn)* *(mōh skoh-shee)*

Some more little words that mean a lot

Fill in the words and say them aloud.

(neh-koh)
neko

_____

tēburu

_____

(ee-noo)
inu

_____

isu

_____

(oo-eh)
ue

_____

(shtah)
shita

_____

See how the parts fit together:

Neko ga, isu no ue ni imasu.

Neko ga,   isu no ue ni imasu.

Cat subject   chair 's top at is
marker

Inu ga, teburu no shita ni imasu.

Inu ga,   tēburu no shita ni imasu.

Dog subject   table 's under at is
marker

Reizōko wa, tēburu no hidari ni arimasu.

left

Isu wa, tēburu no migi ni arimasu.

right

(ah-ee-dah)

Tēburu wa, reizōko to isu no aida ni arimasu.

between

(toh-nah-ree)

Isu wa, tēburu no tonari ni arimasu.

next to

33

(tah-beh-moh-noh)   *(mah-eh)*

Inu no tabemono wa, isu no mae ni arimasu.
   food   front

(oo-shee-roh)

Inu wa, isu no ushiro ni imasu.
         behind

Can you describe where people and things are in this picture?

1. Tanaka san wa, _____ ni imasu.
                             kitchen

2. Reizōko wa, _____ no migi ni arimasu.
                     stove

(mah-tah)

Mata dōshi o
Verbs again

Let's learn some more about verbs. Take another look at a verb we had in the last lesson:

(han-nah-soo)

hanasu (to speak). Now we're adding one more tense: the present continuous. This is the one

that corresponds to the English "ing" form.

PRESENT
(hah-nah-shee-mahs) **hanashimasu**   I speak, you speak, he/she/it speaks, we speak, they speak
PRESENT CONTINUOUS *(hah-nahsh-teh   ee-mahs)* **hanashite**   **imasu**   I am speaking, you are speaking, he/she/it is speaking, we are speaking, they are speaking
PAST *(hah-nah-shee-mahsh-tah)* **hanashimashita**   I spoke, you spoke, he/she/it spoke, we spoke, they spoke
NEGATIVE *(hah-nah-shee-mah-sehn)* **hanashimasen**   I/you don't speak he/she/it doesn't speak, we/they don't speak *(han-nahsh-teh   ee-mah-sehn)* **hanashite**   **imasen**   I'm/you're/he's/she's/it's/we're/they're not speaking *(hah-nah-shee-mah-sehn dehsh-tah)* **hanashimasen**   **deshita**   I/you/he/she/it/we/they didn't speak

In Japanese these tenses usually convey the following meanings:
PRESENT: habitual action (usually, every day, every week, and so forth)
future action (will, going to)
PRESENT CONTINUOUS: immediate action (I'm eating dinner, she's reading, he's sleeping, and so forth)
PAST: completed action: (I went, she said, they saw)
Special uses: Mr. Tanaka comes from Japan. In English, the verb is present tense. In Japanese, "is from" or "comes from" requires a past tense verb.

Tanaka san wa, Nihon kara kimashita.
Japan   from   came

	(mee-roo) **MIRU** to look at, to see	
	AFFIRMATIVE	NEGATIVE
PRESENT	*(mee-mahs)* mimasu	*(mee-mah-sehn)* mimasen
PRESENT CONTINUOUS	*(mee-teh)* mite imasu	mite imasen
PAST	*(mee-mahsh-tah)* mimashita	mimasen deshita

Now fill in the correct verb forms.

(eh)
1. Ano hito tachi ga, e o _____ .
   painting   are looking at

2. Onna no ko ga, otoko no hito ni _____ .
   are talking

Yaku ni tatsu kotoba o mō sukoshi

Some useful words

(eh-gah kahn)
eiga kan
movie theater

(mee-seh)
mise
store

(māh-keht-toh)
māketto
market

(geen-kōh)
ginkō
bank

(yahk-kyoh-koo)
yakkyoku
pharmacy

(mee-chee)
michi
street

(hoh-dōh)
hodō
sidewalk

(kah-oo)
kau
to buy

(shee-mehsh-kah-tah)
Nihongo de no mono no shimeshikata

How to point things out in Japanese

Words like "this" and "that" are important to know, especially when you go shopping and want to point something out. There are three forms in Japanese: one is for something nearby, another for something a short distance away, and another for something at some distance from the speaker. The English equivalents are this, that, and that (over there).

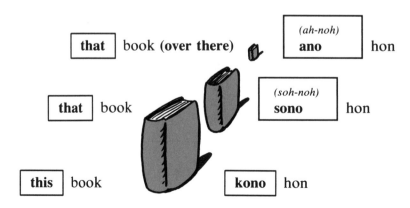

that book (over there)

(ah-noh)
ano hon

that book

(soh-noh)
sono hon

this book

kono hon

You can use the same forms for singular and plural nouns.

Now, try the following: Put the appropriate form of "this/these" "that/those" or "that/those (over there)" in each slot:

1. _____ jidōsha
(jee-dōh-shah)
car

_____ jidōsha

_____ jidōsha

2. _____ neko

_____ neko

_____ neko

It's also helpful to know the words for "here," "there," and "over there."

| here | koko | | there | soko | | over there | asoko |

Where is it?   **Doko desu ka?**   It's here.   **Koko desu.**

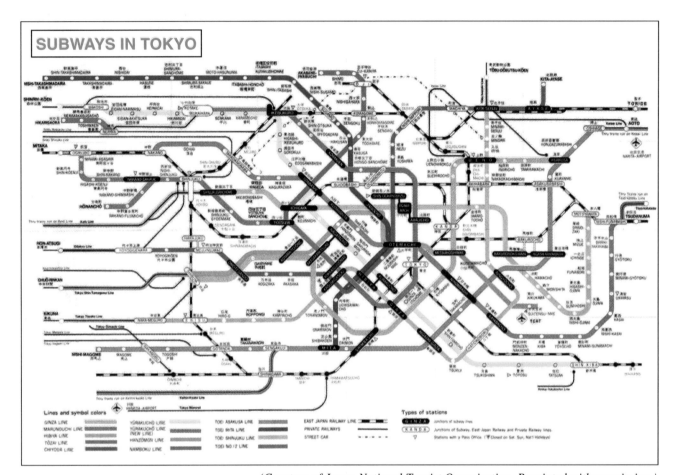

(Courtesy of Japan National Tourist Organization. Reprinted with permission.)

The following dialogue contains some words and expressions that you might find helpful when using public transportation. Read the dialogue carefully several times out loud to familiarize yourself with the meaning and pronunciation of the words.

(geh-KEE-joh) *(tahk-shee)* *(deh)*
MARY   Gekijō made, takushī   de   Shall we take a taxi to the theater?
(ee-kee-mah-shoh)
ikimashō   ka.

(tah-kah-soo-gee-mahs)
MARK   Iie, takasugimasu.   No, it costs too much.

(soh-reh-deh-wah) *(chee-KAH-teh-tsoo)*
MARY   Soredewa,   chikatetsu de   Then let's take the subway.

ikimashō.

38

MARK *(KEHSH-kee)* **Iie, soredewa keshiki ga** *(mee-eh-mah-sehn)* **miemasen.**	No, then I can't see the view.
MARY **Soredewa, basu de ikimashō.**	Well, let's take the bus.
Basu de	On the Bus
MARK *(soo-mee-mah-seh gah)* *(ryōh-keen)* **Sumimasen ga, ryōkin wa** *(EE-koo-rah)* **ikura desu ka.**	Excuse me, sir, how much is the fare?
DRIVER *(hyah-koo roh-KOO-jōō)(ehn)* **Hyaku rokujū en desu.**	One hundred sixty yen.
MARK *(teh-koh-koo)* *(soh-bah)* **Teikoku Gekijō no soba de** *(oh-ree-tah-ee)* **oritai no desu ga.**	We want to get off near the Imperial Theater.
DRIVER *(tsoo-ee-tah-rah)(oh-SHEE-rah-seh)* **Soko ni tsuitara, oshirase shimasu.**	I'll tell you when we get there.
MARK **Arigatō gozaimasu.**	Thank you very much.

Circle the best answer to each question.

1. Merī san wa, _____ *(ee-KEE-tah-ee)* made takushī de ikitai desu.
   wants to go

   a. gekijō   b. hoteru   c. bijutsukan   d. Kyoto

2. Basu no ryōkin wa, _____ desu.
   (nee)
   a. ni hyaku en   b. hyaku en   c. hyaku rokujū en

3. Māku san to Merī san wa, doko de orimasu ka. *(oh-ree-mahs)*
   get off

   (geen-zah)
   a. Ginza de   b. Teikoku Gekijō no soba de   c. kūkō de

Kore wa nan desu ka.

a. Kore wa _____ desu. b. Kore wa _____ desu.

c. Kore wa _____ desu. d. Kore wa _____ desu.

Dōshi o mō sukoshi

More verbs

KAU		
to buy		
	AFFIRMATIVE	NEGATIVE
	(kah-ee-mahs)	(kah-ee-mah-sehn)
PRESENT	kaimasu	kaimasen
	(kaht-teh)	
PRESENT CONTINUOUS	katte imasu	katte imasen
	(kah-ee-mahsh-tah)	
PAST	kaimashita	kaimasen deshita

40

(oh-shee-eh-roo) OSHIERU to teach, to inform, to explain, to tell		
	AFFIRMATIVE	NEGATIVE
PRESENT	(oh-shee-eh-mahs) **oshiemasu**	(oh-shee-eh-mah-sehn) **oshiemasen**
PRESENT CONTINUOUS	(oh-shee-eh-teh) **oshiete imasu**	**oshiete imasen**
PAST	(oh-shee-eh-mahsh-tah) **oshiemashita**	**oshiemasen deshita**

(ee-koo) IKU to go		
	AFFIRMATIVE	NEGATIVE
PRESENT	**ikimasu**	(ee-kee-mah-sehn) **ikimasen**
PRESENT CONTINUOUS	(eet-teh) **itte imasu**	**itte imasen**
PAST	(ee-kee-mahsh-tah) **ikimashita**	**ikimasen deshita**

BASU NO UNTENSHU TO HANASU
(oon-tehn-shoo) (toh)
Speaking with the Bus Driver

Here are some phrases to help you communicate with the bus driver.

(noh-roo)
noru   to get on, to ride on

(oh-ree-roo)
oriru   to get off

(noh-ree-kah-eh-roo)
norikaeru   to transfer

(kōh-kah)
kōka   coins

(tēh-ryoo-joh)
basu no tēryūjo   bus stop

basu no untenshu   bus driver

Ginza e no ryōkin wa, ikura desu ka.   How much is the fare to Ginza?

Here are the **verbs** that were just introduced:

NORU		
to get on, to ride on		
	AFFIRMATIVE	NEGATIVE
	(noh-ree-mahs)	*(noh-ree-mah-sehn)*
PRESENT	norimasu	norimasen
	(noht-teh)	
PRESENT CONTINUOUS	notte imasu	notte imasen
	(noh-ree-mahsh-tah)	
PAST	norimashita	norimasen deshita

ORIRU		
to get off		
	AFFIRMATIVE	NEGATIVE
	(oh-ree-mahs)	*(oh-ree-mah-sehn)*
PRESENT	orimasu	orimasen
	(oh-ree-teh)	
PRESENT CONTINUOUS	orite imasu	orite imasen
	(oh-ree-mahsh-tah)	
PAST	orimashita	orimasen deshita

NORIKAERU		
to transfer		
	AFFIRMATIVE	NEGATIVE
	(noh-ree-kah-eh-mahs)	*(noh-ree-kah-eh-mah-sehn)*
PRESENT	norikaemasu	norikaemasen
	(noh-ree-kah-eh-teh)	
PRESENT CONTINUOUS	norikaete imasu	norikaete imasen
	(noh-ree-kah-eh-mahsh-tah)	
PAST	norikaemashita	norikaemasen deshita

Now read the following paragraph about Mark and Mary going to Ginza.

Māku san to Merī san wa, Amerika kara kimashita. Karera wa ima, Tokyo ni imasu. Basu de,
(shohp-peen-goo)   *(yohn-chōh-meh)*
Ginza e ikimasu. Shoppingu ni ikitai desu. Ginza Yonchōme no kōsaten de basu o orimasu.

Can you answer these questions based on the paragraph? Write the Japanese in the spaces provided, then check your answers below.

1. Māku san to Merī san wa, doko kara kimashita ka.

---

2. Karera wa ima, doko ni imasu ka.

_____

3. Basu de, doko e ikimasu ka.

_____

4. Shoppingu ni ikitai desu ka.

_____

5. Doko de basu o orimasu ka.

_____

Joshi ni tsuite mō sukoshi

More about particles

Earlier we saw how particles—short words which come *after* other words—are important in Japanese. They help to identify the relationship of the word they follow to other parts of the sentence.

By now you're probably familiar with **ka**—the particle that's used at the end of a question. And you're beginning to feel more comfortable with the particles such as **ni**, **e**, and **de**, which are like the English prepositions, ''in,'' ''to,'' and ''at.''

Let's take a closer look at a few others.

Wa and **ga** are both called subject markers. More accurately, **wa** is a topic marker, and **ga** is the grammatical subject marker. Sometimes a sentence can have both.

When you're learning Japanese, choosing between the **wa** and **ga** can be a bit of a challenge. For now, just observe how they're used in the sentences in these lessons, and you'll soon get a feel for **wa** and **ga**.

O is the object marker. It's used after the grammatical object of the sentence. Sometimes, for emphasis, **ga** may be used as an object marker.

No is the possessive marker. It expresses both possession and the ''of the'' meaning in English. Let's see how it works:

tēboru	**no**	ue	the top of the table
kare	**no**	hon	his book
Māku san	**no**	okusan	Mark's wife
watakushi	**no**	kuruma	my car
basu	**no**	untenshu	bus driver (driver of the bus)

This exercise will help you check your knowledge of particles. For each item, fill in the missing particle or particles.

1. Māku san _____ , Amerika kara kimashita.

2. Kare _____ okusan _____ Tokyo ni imasu.

(hah-nah-seh-mah-sehn)
3. Pōru san _____ Nihongo _____ hanasemasen.
can't speak

4. Ryōkin _____ ikura desu _____ .

5. Jirō san _____ , pan _____ katte imasu.

Now let's do the same for the particles that function like English prepositions.

1. Jirō san wa, mainichi gakkō _____ ikimasu.

2. Neko ga, tēburu no shita _____ imasu.

3. Merī san wa, Ginza _____ imasu.

4. Māku san wa, Ginza _____ basu o orimasu.

5. Tanaka san wa, Nihon _____ kimashita.

-tai
want to

Here's a useful expression that will enable you to say "want to" with verbs. Start with the present tense form of the verb. Remove the **-masu** and replace it with **-tai**. Then add **desu**.

It looks like this:

ikimasu	go	**ikitai desu**	want to go
		(kah-ee-tah-ee)	
kaimasu	buy	**kaitai desu**	want to buy
		(mee-tah-ee)	
mimasu	see	**mitai desu**	want to see

Kyoto ni ikitai desu.   I want to go to Kyoto.
Pōru san wa, pan o kaitai desu.   Paul wants to buy bread.
Merī san wa, heya o mitai desu.   Mary wants to see the room.

Isn't that easy? Now try a few yourself!

1. Shoppingu ni _____ .   (want to go)

2. Basu no untenshu ni _____ .   (want to speak)

3. Merī san wa, takushī de _____ .   (wants to go)

4. Watakushi wa, Nihongo o _____ .   (want to speak)

5. Māku san wa, bijutsukan o _____ .   (wants to see)

ANSWERS

Want to   1. ikitai desu   2. hanashitai desu   3. ikitai desu   4. hanashitai desu   5. mitai desu

5	*(jee-kahn)* # Jikan to kazu *(kah-zoo)* Time and Numbers		

The Japanese language is rich in numbers. It uses Japanese numbers and Chinese numbers. And it uses a system of classifiers or "counters" as well. This means that when you count things, you first have to classify them according to what they are, or by their size or shape. For example, to count pencils, bottles, or trees, you use the classifier for long, thin things; to count books or magazines, you use the classifier for bound objects. Later in this lesson you'll see a chart of some of the most common classifiers.

(kee-sōo)
KISŪ
Cardinal Numbers

From 1 to 10 only, there are two sets of numbers. The set on the right, of Japanese origin, stops at 10. The set on the left, of Chinese origin, continues indefinitely.

(ee-chee) **ichi**	1	*(hee-toh-tsoo)* **hitotsu**	
(nee) **ni**	2	*(foo-tah-tsoo)* **futatsu**	
(sahn) **san**	3	*(meet-tsoo)* **mittsu**	
(shee) (yohn) **shi/yon**	4	*(yoht-tsoo)* **yottsu**	
(goh) **go**	5	*(ee-tsoo-tsoo)* **itsutsu**	
(roh-koo) **roku**	6	*(moot-tsoo)* **muttsu**	
(shee-chee) (nah-nah) **shichi/nana**	7	*(nah-nah-tsoo)* **nanatsu**	
(hah-chee) **hachi**	8	*(yaht-tsoo)* **yattsu**	
(koo) (kyōo) **ku/kyū**	9	*(koh-koh-noh-tsoo)* **kokonotsu**	
(jōo) **jū**	10	*(tōh)* **tō**	

To form numbers from 11 to 19, start with **jū**, 10, and then add the number you need from the column on the *left*:

11 **jū ichi**   12 **jū ni**   13 **jū san**   14 **jū shi/yon**   15 **jū go**
16 **jū roku**   17 **jū shichi/nana**   18 **jū hachi**   19 **jū ku**

The rest is easy. Twenty is two tens, or **ni jū**, and for 21, just add the 1: **ni jū ichi**.

20 **ni jū**	30 **san jū**	40 **yon jū**	50 **go jū**
21 **ni jū ichi**	31 **san jū ichi**	41 **yon jū ichi**	51 **go jū ichi**

| 60 roku jū | 70 nana jū | 80 hachi jū | 90 kyū jū |
| 61 roku jū ichi | 71 nana jū ichi | 81 hachi jū ichi | 91 kyū jū ichi |

With 100, **hyaku**, *(hyah-koo)* and 1000, **sen**, *(sehn)* the pattern is basically the same, but there are some sound changes:

100	**hyaku**	1,000	**sen**
200	**ni hyaku**	2,000	**ni sen**
300	**san byaku** *(byah-koo)*	3,000	**san zen** *(zehn)*
400	**yon hyaku**	4,000	**yon sen**
500	**go hyaku**	5,000	**go sen**
600	**roppyaku** *(rohp-pyah-koo)*	6,000	**roku sen**
700	**nana hyaku**	7,000	**nana sen**
800	**happyaku** *(hahp-pyah-koo)*	8,000	**hassen** *(hahs-sehn)*
900	**kyū hyaku**	9,000	**kyū sen**

Japanese uses 10,000 as a counting unit. Each unit of 10,000 is called **man**. *(mahn)* So 10,000 is

ichi man, 20,000 is **ni man**, 100,000 is **jū man**, 200,000 is **ni jū man**, 1,000,000 is **hyaku man** (100

units of 10,000). This continues until 100,000,000, **ichi oku**. *(oh-koo)*

Can you say the following numbers in Japanese? Write the words next to each:

1. 16 _____

2. 23 _____

3. 37 _____

4. 54 _____

5. 78 _____

6. 82 _____

7. 101 _____

8. 704 _____

9. 6,500 _____

10. 30,000 _____

47

Josū
Ordinal numbers

	(bahn meh)		
First	**ichi ban me**	Sixth	**roku ban me**
Second	**ni ban me**	Seventh	**nana ban me**
Third	**san ban me**	Eighth	**hachi ban me**
Fourth	**yon ban me**	Ninth	**kyū ban me**
Fifth	**go ban me**	Tenth	**jū ban me**

To continue, follow the pattern for the cardinal numbers, adding "**ban me.**" Eleventh is **jū ichi ban me**, twelfth is **jū ni ban me**, and so forth.

(nahn-jee)
NANJI DESU KA
What time is it?

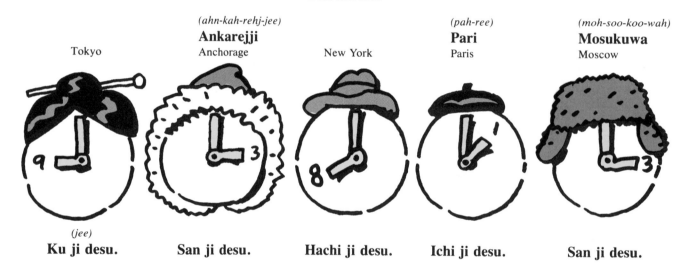

Tokyo	*(ahn-kah-rehj-jee)* **Ankarejji** Anchorage	New York	*(pah-ree)* **Pari** Paris	*(moh-soo-koo-wah)* **Mosukuwa** Moscow

(jee)
Ku ji desu.   **San ji desu.**   **Hachi ji desu.**   **Ichi ji desu.**   **San ji desu.**

To express time in Japanese, we start with a list of the **hours**, then a list of the **minutes**, and then we'll put them together.

Here are the **hours:**

1 o'clock	**ichi ji**	7 o'clock	**shichi ji**
2 o'clock	**ni ji**	8 o'clock	**hachi ji**
3 o'clock	**san ji**	9 o'clock	**ku ji**
4 o'clock	*(yoh)* **yo ji**	10 o'clock	**jū ji**
5 o'clock	**go ji**	11 o'clock	*(jōo-ee-chee)* **jūichi ji**
6 o'clock	**roku ji**	12 o'clock	*(jōo-nee)* **juni ji**

Now the **minutes**:

1 minute	*(eep-poon)* **ippun**		11 minutes	**jū ippun**
2 minutes	*(foon)* **ni fun**		12 minutes	**jū ni fun**
3 minutes	*(poon)* **san pun**		13 minutes	**jū san pun**
4 minutes	**yon pun**		14 minutes	**jū yon pun**
5 minutes	**go fun**		15 minutes	**jū go fun**
6 minutes	*(rohp-poon)* **roppun**		16 minutes	**jū roppun**
7 minutes	**nana fun**		17 minutes	**jū nana fun**
8 minutes	*(hahp-poon)* **happun**		18 minutes	**jū happun**
9 minutes	**kyū fun**		19 minutes	**jū kyū fun**
10 minutes	*(joop-poon)* **juppun**		20 minutes	**ni juppun**

21 minutes	**ni jū ippun**
22 minutes	**ni jū ni fun**
23 minutes	**ni jū san pun**
24 minutes	**ni jū yon pun**
25 minutes	**ni jū go fun**
30 minutes	**san juppun**
40 minutes	**yon juppun**
50 minutes	**go juppun**

Now let's put them together. Say the hour first, then the minutes, then add **desu**. For example:

Nanji desu ka.   What time is it?
Jū ji jū go fun desu.   It's 10:15.

(soo-gee)
Using **sugi**, which means "past" or "after," is optional.

Jū ji jū go fun sugi desu.   It's 10:15.

49

At 15 minutes before the hour, start using **mae**, which means "to" or "before."

Jū ji jū go fun **mae** desu.   It's a quarter to ten.

(hahn)
Han means "half," as in half past the hour.

Go ji desu.	It's 5 o'clock.
Go ji go fun desu.	It's 5:05.
Go ji juppun desu.	It's 5:10.
Go ji jū go fun desu.	It's 5:15.
Go ji ni juppun desu.	It's 5:20.
Go ji ni jū go fun desu.	It's 5:25.
Go ji han desu.	It's 5:30.
Go ji san jū go fun desu.	It's 5:35.
Go ji yon juppun desu.	It's 5:40.
Go ji yon jū go fun desu.	It's 5:45.
Roku ji jū go fun mae desu.	It's a quarter to six.
Roku ji juppun mae desu.	It's 5:50/ten to six.
Roku ji go fun mae desu.	It's 5:55/five to six.

(goh-zehn)   *(goh-goh)*
Gozen is "AM", **gogo** is "PM." Say them *before* you say the hour.

Gozen ku ji desu.   It's 9 AM.
Gogo jū ji desu.   It's 10 PM.

For time schedules, as in railway and airline timetables, numbers 1 to 59 are used for minutes, *not* "a quarter to" or "ten to" the hour.

Transportation timetables are based on the 24-hour clock. Airline and train schedules are expressed in terms of a point within a 24-hour sequence.

(kee-shah)   *(deh-mahs)*
Watakushi no kisha wa, **jū san ji yon jū happun** ni demasu.
    My train departs at **13:48 (1:48 PM)**.

Watakushi no hikōki wa, **jū ji go jū san pun** ni tsukimasu.
    My plane arrives at **10:53 (AM)**.

Now look at the clocks. Can you tell the time in Japanese? Write your answers in the space provided.

1. _____   2. _____   3. _____

4. _____   5. _____

And, remember, if you want to count things, you need to use those special **classifiers**, or **counters**. Here are some of the most common ones and a few examples to show you how they're used.

(chee-gaht-tah)   *(shoo-roo-ee)*   *(kah-zoh-eh-roo)*
Chigatta shurui no mono o kazoeru
Counting different kinds of things

One American is coming.
  Amerikajin ga **hitori** kimasu.
  American   one

One pencil is on the table.
  Enpitsu ga **ippon** tēburu no ue ni arimasu.
  pencil   one

I have one book.
  Hon o **issatsu** motte imasu.
  book   one

I'd like one ticket.
  Ken o **ichimai** kudasai.
  ticket   one

people

(hee-toh-ree)	
1. **hitori**	4. **yo nin**
(foo-tah-ree)	
2. **futari**	5. **go nin**
(neen)	
3. **san nin**	

long, thin objects (pencils, bottles, trees)

(eep-pohn)	
1. **ippon**	4. **yon hon**
(hohn)	
2. **ni hon**	5. **go hon**
(bohn)	
3. **san bon**	

bound objects (books, notebooks, magazines)

(ees-sah-tsoo)	
1. **issatsu**	4. **yon satsu**
(sah-tsoo)	
2. **ni satsu**	5. **go satsu**
(sah-tsoo)	
3. **san satsu**	

thin, flat objects (paper, bills, cloth, tickets, dishes)

(mah-ee)	
1. **ichi mai**	4. **yon mai**
2. **ni mai**	5. **go mai**
3. **san mai**	

liquid or dry measures (glasses or cups of water, coffee or tea)

(eep-pah-ee)	
1. **ippai**	4. **yon hai**
(hah-ee)	
2. **ni hai**	5. **go hai**
(bah-ee)	
3. **san bai**	

houses, buildings

(eek-kehn)
1. **ikken**

4. **yon ken**

(kehn)
2. **ni ken**

5. **go ken**

(gehn)
3. **san gen**

small objects not in the categories above

(eek-koh) (hee-toh-tsoo)
1. **ikko / hitotsu**

(yoht-tsoo)
4. **yon ko / yottsu**

(koh) (foo-tah-tsoo)
2. **ni ko / futatsu**

(ee-tsoo-tsoo)
5. **go ko / itsutsu**

(meet-tsoo)
3. **san ko / mittsu**

floors of buildings

(eek-kah-ee)
1. **ikkai**

(rohk-kah-ee)
6. **rokkai**

(kah-ee)
2. **ni kai**

7. **nana kai**

(gah-ee)
3. **san gai**

(hahk-kah-ee)
8. **hakkai**

4. **yon kai**

9. **kyū kai**

5. **go kai**

(jook-kah-ee)
10. **jukkai**

If you were in an elevator in a building in Japan, how would you ask for your floor? Remember to use the numbers with the proper counter, *not* the ordinal numbers.

1. second floor _____

4. ninth floor _____

2. fifth floor _____

5. tenth floor _____

3. sixth floor _____

Now back to the time! Here's a dialogue for you to read aloud several times.

STRANGER	**Chotto sumimasen ga,**	Excuse me, sir, what time is it?
	nanji desu ka.	
MARK	*(hee-roo) (goh-roh)* **Hiru goro da to omoimasu.**	I think it's around noon.
STRANGER	*(toh-keh) (ee-nah-ee)* **Tokei o, motte inai**	Don't you have a watch?
	no desu ka.	
MARK	**Hai, motte imasen.**	*Yes, I don't have a watch.
STRANGER	*(kyah-koo)* **Kankō kyaku desu ka.**	Are you a tourist?
MARK	*(soh)* **Hai, sō desu.**	Yes, I am.
STRANGER	*(ee-ree-mahs)* **Tokei ga, irimasu yo.**	You need a watch!
MARK	*(wah-kaht-teh) (deh-moh)* **Wakatte imasu. Demo,** *(noo-soo-mah-reh-teh)* **tokei o nusumarete** *(shee-mah-ee-mahsh-tah)* **shimaimashita.**	I know. But my watch was stolen.
STRANGER	*(nah-ee)* **Nihon de dewa nai** *(deh-shoh)* **desho.**	Not in Japan, was it?
MARK	**Hai. Koko ni tsuku** **mae desu.**	*Yes. Before we arrived here.
STRANGER	**Nihon de, ii tokei** *(kah-eh-mahs)* **ga kaemasu yo.**	You can buy a good watch here in Japan.
MARK	*(tsoo-moh-ree)* **Kau tsumori desu.**	I will.

* Notice that, unlike English, a negative question (Don't you?) gets a positive answer (Yes, I don't).

Can you write these phrases from the dialogue in Japanese?

1. What time is it? _____

2. I think it's around noon. _____

3. Are you a tourist? _____

(oh-boh-eh-teh)

Oboete imasu ka
Remember

Remember the saying, "If it's Tuesday, I must be in . . ."

(geh-tsoo yoh-bee) | *(kah)* | *(soo-ee)* | *(moh-koo)* **moku yōbi** | *(keen)* | *(doh)* **do yōbi** | *(nee-chee)*
getsu yōbi | **ka yōbi** | **sui yōbi** | | **kin yōbi** | | **nichi yōbi**

kyō
today

(kee-nōh)
kinō
yesterday

ashita
tomorrow

mata
again

(mah-dah)
mada
still, yet

(ee-tsoo-moh)
itsumo
always

mo
also, too

Now see if you remember the meaning of the following adverbs by matching them up with their English equivalents.

1. **kyō**   a. today
2. **kinō**   b. still
3. **ashita**   c. again
4. **itsumo**   d. also
5. **mata**   e. tomorrow
6. **mada**   f. always
7. **mo**   g. yesterday

If you need to take the train, the following dialogue might prove useful to you. Don't forget to read it aloud.

MARK	*(eh-kee)* *(tskee-mahsh-tah)* **Eki ni tsukimashita yo.**	Here we are at the train station.
ANNE	*(sheen-kahn-sehn)* **Otōsan, shinkansen ni** **notte Kyōto e iku no.**	Dad, are we taking the bullet train to go to Kyoto?
MARK	*(keep-poo)* *(oo-ree-bah)* **Sō da yo. (kippu uriba** *(kah-kah-ree-een)* **no kakariin ni) Sumimasen ga.** *(ōh-fkoo)* *(kehn)* **Kyōto yuki no ōfuku ken wa,** *(boon)* **yonin bun ikura desu ka.**	Yes. (to the ticket clerk) Excuse me. How much does a round-trip ticket to Kyoto for four people cost?
CLERK	**Shinkansen de desu ka.**	By super-express?
MARK	**Hai, sō desu.**	Yes.

56

CLERK **Teisha ga sukunai hayai** *(teh-shah) (skoo-nah-ee) (hah-yah-ee)* **kisha ga ii desu ka. Soretomo** *(soh-reh-toh-moh)* **teisha ga ōi osoi kisha ga** *(oh-ee) (oh-soh-ee)* **ii desu ka.**	Do you want the faster train with fewer stops, or the slower train with more stops?
MARK **Hayai kisha o onegai** *(oh-neh-gah-ee)* **shimasu.** *(shee-mahs)*	The faster one, please.
CLERK **Hayai kisha wa, "Hikari"** **desu. Gurīn sha ga ii desu** *(goo-rēen) (shah)* **ka. Futsū ga ii desu ka.** *(foo-tsoo)*	That's called the Hikari. Do you want first class or regular?
MARK **Futsū o onegai shimasu.**	Regular.
CLERK **Shitei seki ni shimasu** *(shteh) (seh-kee)* **ka, jiyū seki ni shimasu ka.** *(jee-YOO)*	Reserved seats or unreserved seats?
MARK **Shitei seki o, onegai** **shimasu.**	Reserved seats, please.
CLERK **Kitsuen seki ga ii desu** *(kee-TSOO-ehn)* **ka, kinen seki ga ii desu ka.** *(keen-ehn)*	Smoking or nonsmoking section?
MARK **Kinen seki o onegai** **shimasu.**	Nonsmoking.
CLERK **Zenbu de, jū man happyaku** *(zehn-boo)* **en desu.**	The total is 100,800 yen.
MARK **Arigatō. Kisha wa, nanji** **ni demasu ka.**	Thank you. What time does the train leave?
CLERK **Kuji han desu.**	At 9:30.

Match these Japanese words or expressions from the dialogue with their English equivalents.

1. kinen seki
2. shitei seki
3. ōfuku ken
4. eki
5. gurīn sha

a. first class
b. round-trip ticket
c. train station
d. nonsmoking section
e. reserved seats

Japan has an efficient rail system. The **Shinkansen**, popularly known as the bullet train, or super-express, operated by Japan Railways (JR), is a convenient way to travel. There are many other types of passenger trains as well.

There are four Shinkansen lines. Some lines have different kinds of trains, faster ones with fewer stops, and slower ones with more stops, as you can see on the chart. You can specify the one you want when buying your ticket.

(tōh-kah-ee-dōh) (sahn-yōh) **TOKAIDO-SANYO SHINKANSEN**		*(tōh-hoh-koo) (yah-mah-gah-tah)* **TOHOKU-YAMAGATA SHINKANSEN**	
Route	*(hah-kah-tah)* Tokyo station, Tokyo—Hakata	**Route**	*(moh-ree-oh-kah)* Tokyo Station, Tokyo—Morioka
Fewest stops	*(noh-zoh-mee)* Nozomi trains	**Fewer stops**	*(yah-mah-bee-koh)* Yamabiko trains
More stops	*(hee-kah-ree)* Hikari trains	**More stops**	*(ah-oh-bah)* Aoba trains
Most stops	*(koh-dah-mah)* Kodama trains	**Route**	Tokyo Station, Tokyo—Yamagata
			(tsoo-bah-sah) Tsubasa trains
(jōh-eh-tsoo) **JOETSU SHINKANSEN**		*(hoh-koo-ree-koo)* **HOKURIKU SHINKANSEN**	
Route	*(neē-gah-tah)* Tokyo Station, Tokyo—Niigata	**Route**	*(nah-gah-noh)* Tokyo Station, Tokyo—Nagano
Fewer stops	*(ah-sah-hee)* Asahi trains		*(ah-sah-mah)* Asama trains
More stops	*(toh-kee)* Toki trains		

Other Types of Trains

	(tohk-kyōō)
Limited express	**tokkyū**
	(kyōō-koh)
Ordinary express	**kyūkō**
	(foo-tsōō)
Local trains	**futsū**

Fares and Classes

You need a basic fare ticket for all train travel. And if you travel by Shinkansen, limited express, or ordinary express, you pay a supplementary fare as well. There are three classes of seats on these trains: Green car (first class), reserved seats, and unreserved seats. Green car and reserved seats also cost extra.

When traveling on intercity trains in Japan, you should buy your tickets in advance. Trains are popular, and choice seats fill up fast. Check with a travel agency, and get the train and class you want. You can, of course, buy tickets at the station as well.

Before you depart for Japan, you might want to inquire at your local All Nippon Airways (ANA) or Japan Air Lines (JAL) ticket office about the money-saving Japan Rail Pass.

An important note: there are few porters in Japanese train stations, and there may be many stairs to climb. You'll do well to travel light!

(nah-nee-kah)   (tah-noh-moo)

Nanika o tanomu
Asking for something

We've already seen that you can express ''want'' with a verb by deleting the **-masu** and
(tah-ee)
replacing it with **-tai**. Thus **ikimasu** is ''go,'' and **ikitai** is ''want to go.''
(hoh-shēē)
To express ''want'' with nouns, use **hoshii desu** at the end, and use **ga** as the object marker (instead of the usual **o**).

Kōhī ga hoshii desu.	I want some coffee.
Shinbun ga hoshii desu.	I want a newspaper.

You can achieve the same thing with the expression for ''give me.'' Use **kudasai** at the end, and use **o** with the object as usual.

Hon o kudasai.	Give me a book.
Ōfuku ken o kudasai.	Give me a round-trip ticket.

Note: although the English equivalents above sound abrupt, in Japanese they aren't. The "please" is implied.

Another option is the expression for "please." Use **onegai shimasu** at the end of the sentence, and use **o** with the object.

Gurīn sha o onegai shimasu.	(Give me/I want) first class, please.
(oh-chah)	
Ocha o onegai shimasu.	(Give me/I want) some tea, please.

Can you match the Japanese with the English equivalents?

1. Kanojo wa Kyoto ni ikitai desu.

2. Kōhī o onegai shimasu.

3. Hon o kaitai desu.

4. Pan ga hoshii desu.

5. Isu o kudasai.

a. I want to buy some books.

b. She wants to go to Kyoto.

c. Some coffee, please.

d. Give me a chair.

e. I want some bread.

(joh-shah)
JŌSHA
All Aboard!

(joh-kyah-koo)
jōkyaku
passenger

(soo-wah-roo)
suwaru
to sit

(tah-tsoo)
tatsu
to stand

(mah-chee-ah-ee-shtsoo)
machiaishitsu
waiting room

(skeh-joo-roo)
sukejūru
schedule

(poo-raht-toh-hoh-moo)
purattohōmu
railway platform

(kee-shah)
kisha
train

61

Here are the **verbs** that were just introduced:

	(soo-wah-roo) **SUWARU** to sit	
	AFFIRMATIVE	NEGATIVE
PRESENT	*(soo-wah-ree-mahs)* **suwarimasu**	*(soo-wah-ree-mah-sehn)* **suwarimasen**
PRESENT CONTINUOUS	*(soo-waht-teh)* **suwatte imasu**	**suwatte imasen**
PAST	*(soo-wah-ree-mahsh-tah)* **suwarimashita**	**suwarimasen deshita**

	(tah-tsoo) **TATSU** to stand	
	AFFIRMATIVE	NEGATIVE
PRESENT	*(tah-chee-mahs)* **tachimasu**	*(tah-chee-mah-sehn)* **tachimasen**
PRESENT CONTINUOUS	*(taht-teh)* **tatte imasu**	**tatte imasen**
PAST	*(tah-chee-mahsh-tah)* **tachimashita**	**tachimasen deshita**

and some useful new ones:

	(kee-koo) **KIKU** to ask, to listen to, to hear	
	AFFIRMATIVE	NEGATIVE
PRESENT	*(kee-kee-mahs)* **kikimasu**	*(kee-kee-mah-sehn)* **kikimasen**
PRESENT CONTINUOUS	*(kee-ee-teh)* **kiite imasu**	**kiite imasen**
PAST	*(kee-kee-mahsh-tah)* **kikimashita**	**kikimasen deshita**

	(soo-roo) **SURU** to do	
	AFFIRMATIVE	NEGATIVE
PRESENT	*(shee-mahs)* **shimasu**	*(shee-mah-sehn)* **shimasen**
PRESENT CONTINUOUS	**shite imasu**	**shite imasen**
PAST	*(shee-mahsh-tah)* **shimashita**	**shimasen deshita**

Jibun de shinasai

(jee-boon) *(shee-nah-sah-ee)*

Do it yourself

In English, such words as "myself," "yourself," and "himself" are called reflexive pronouns. In Japanese, you express the same meaning with the word **jibun**, which means "one's self," and can be considered an all-purpose reflexive pronoun.

Jibun de ikimasu.	I'm going myself.
Kanojo wa jibun de shite imasu.	She's doing it herself.
Merī san wa, jibun de shoppingu ni ikitai desu.	Mary wants to go shopping herself.

The following passage is about train travel. Read about Mark and Mary, then answer the questions.

Māku san to Merī san wa, Tokyo eki ni imasu. Karera wa, Tokyo kara Osaka e no ōfuku ken o kaimashita. Gurīn sha de ikimasu. Kisha wa, saisho ni Nagoya to Kyoto e ikimasu. Gogo shichi ji ni, Osaka ni tsukimasu.

1. Māku san to Merī san wa, doko ni imasu ka.
2. Nani o kaimashita ka.
3. Kisha wa, saisho ni doko e ikimasu ka.

ANSWERS

Reading 1. Tokyo eki ni imasu. 2. Tokyo kara Osaka e no ōfuku ken o kaimashita. 3. Kisha wa, saisho ni Nagoya to Kyoto e ikimasu.

(skoh-shee)

Watakushi wa, Nihongo o sukoshi hanashimasu. I speak a little Japanese. And so do you! By now you've learned quite a bit of Japanese. Take a look at the rest of the world too, and learn how to say the names of other countries in Japanese.

Argentina	*(ah-roo-zehn-cheen)* **Aruzenchin**	Chile	*(chee-ree)* **Chiri**
Australia	*(oh-stoh-rah-ree-ah)* **Ōsutoraria**	China	*(choo-goh-koo)* **Chūgoku**
Austria	*(oh-stoh-ree-ah)* **Ōsutoria**	Denmark	*(dehn-mah-koo)* **Denmāku**
Belgium	*(beh-roo-gee)* **Berugī**	Egypt	*(eh-jee-poo-toh)* **Ejiputo**
Brazil	*(boo-rah-jee-roo)* **Buirajiru**	England	*(ee-gee-ree-soo)* **Igirisu**
Canada	*(kah-nah-dah)* **Kanada**	France	*(foo-rahn-soo)* **Furansu**

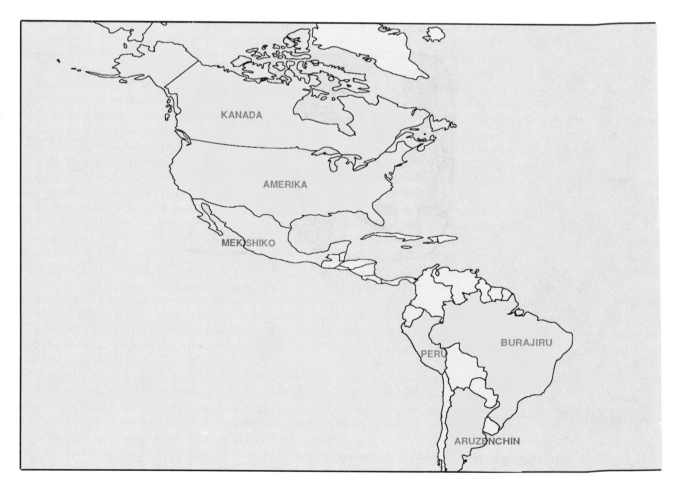

Germany	*(doh-ee-tsoo)* **Doitsu**	New Zealand	*(nyōo-jēe-rahn-doh)* **Nyūzīrando**
Holland	*(oh-rahn-dah)* **Oranda**	Norway	*(noh-roo-weh̄)* **Noruwē**
India	*(een-doh)* **Indo**	Pakistan	*(pah-kees-tahn)* **Pakisutan**
Indonesia	*(een-doh-neh-shee-ah)* **Indoneshia**	Philippines	*(fee-ree-peen)* **Firipin**
Iran	*(ee-rahn)* **Iran**	Poland	*(pōh-rahn-doh)* **Pōrando**
Italy	*(ee-tah-ree-ah)* **Itaria**	Portugal	*(poh-roo-toh-gah-roo)* **Porutogaru**
Japan	*(nee-hohn)* **Nihon**	Russia	*(roh-shee-ah)* **Roshia**
Korea	*(kahn-koh-koo)* **Kankoku**	Saudi Arabia	*(sah-oo-jee ah-rah-bee-ah)* **Sauji Arabia**
Malaysia	*(mah-reh̄-shee-ah)* **Marēshia**	Singapore	*(sheen-gah-pōh-roo)* **Shingapōru**
Mexico	*(meh-kee-shee-koh)* **Mekishiko**	South Africa	*(mee-nah-mee ah-foo-ree-kah)* **Minami Afurika**
Myanmar	*(myahn-mah̄)* **Myanmā**	Spain	*(soo-peh-een)* **Supein**

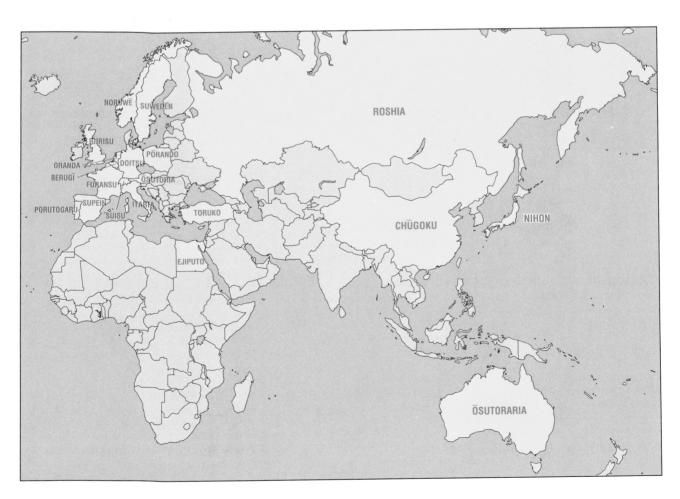

Sweden	*(soo-wēh-dehn)* **Suwēden**	Turkey	*(toh-roo-koh)* **Toruko**
Switzerland	*(soo-ee-soo)* **Suisu**	United States	*(ah-meh-ree-kah)* **Amerika**
Thailand	*(tah-ee-koh-koo)* **Taikoku**	Vietnam	*(beh-toh-nah-moo)* **Betonamu**

Kotoba
Languages

Watakushi wa Nihongo o hanashimasu.
Japanese

(doh-ee-tsoo-goh)
Watakushi wa Doitsugo o hanashimasu.
German

Watakushi wa Furansugo o hanashimasu.
French

Watakushi wa Chūgokugo o hanashimasu.
Chinese

Watakushi wa Supeingo o hanashimasu.
Spanish

(roh-shee-ah-go)
Watakushi wa Roshiago o hanashimasu.
Russian

(ēh-goh)
Watakushi wa eigo o hanashimasu.
English

Watakushi wa Itariago o hanashimasu.
Italian

(kohk-seh-kee)
Kokuseki
Nationalities

(jeen)
To express nationality, just add **jin** to the name of the country.

Watakushi wa, <u>Amerikajin</u> desu.   I'm <u>American</u>.

(ōh-stoh-rah-ree-ah-jeen)
Ōsutorariajin

(ōh-stoh-ree-ah-jeen)
Ōsutoriajin

(beh-roo-gēē-jeen)
Berugījin

(ee-gee-ree-soo-jeen)
Igirisujin

(kah-nah-dah-jeen)
Kanadajin

(chōō-goh-koo-jeen)
Chūgokujin

(dehn-māh-koo-jeen)
Denmākujin

(oh-rahn-dah-jeen)
Orandajin

(foo-rahn-soo-jeen)
Furansujin

(doh-ee-tsoo-jeen)
Doitsujin

(ee-tah-ree-ah-jeen)
Itariajin

(nee-hohn-jeen)
Nihonjin

(meh-kee-shee-koh-jeen)
Mekishikojin

(noh-roo-wēh-jeen)
Noruwējin

(pōh-rahn-doh-jeen)
Pōrandojin

(roh-shee-ah-jeen)
Roshiajin

(soo-peh-een-jeen)
Supeinjin

(soo-wēh-dehn-jeen)
Suwēdenjin

(soo-ee-soo-jeen)
Suisujin

(toh-roo-koh-jeen)
Torukojin

. . . e ikimasu

I'm going to . . .

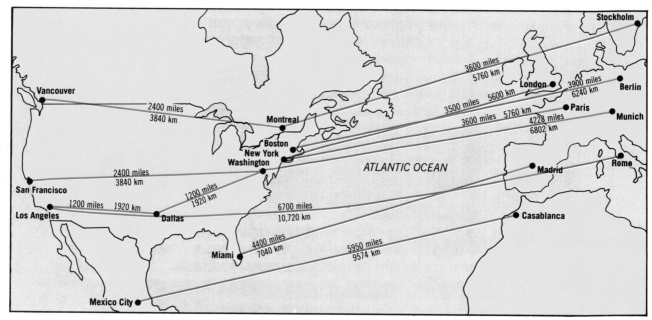

Let's place some cities in their proper countries:

Nyūyōku wa doko ni arimasu ka. (Amerika)

   Nyūyōku wa Amerika ni arimasu.

(bahn-kōo-bāh)

1. Bankūbā wa doko ni arimasu ka. (Kanada)

_____

(soo-tohk-koo-hoh-roo-moo)

2. Sutokkuhorumu wa doko ni arimasu ka. (Suwēden)

_____

3. Pari wa doko ni arimasu ka. (Furansu)

_____

(mah-doh-reed-doh)

4. Madoriddo wa doko ni arimasu ka. (Supein)

_____

(rohn-dohn)

5. Rondon wa doko ni arimasu ka. (Igirisu)

_____

ANSWERS

Cities   1. Bankūbā wa Kanada ni arimasu. **2.** Sutokkuhorumu wa Suwēden ni arimasu. **3.** Pari wa Furansu ni arimasu. **4.** Madoriddo wa Supein ni arimasu. **5.** Rondon wa Igirisu ni arimasu.

(nah-koo-shtah) *(hahn-doh-bahg-goo)*

Nakushita handobaggu

A lost purse

Can you imagine how Anne feels when, during a day of shopping and sightseeing, she discovers she has lost her purse? She stops a policeman on a busy Tokyo street.

(tah-skeh-teh)

ANNE **Sumimasen ga, tasukete**

itadakemasu ka.

Excuse me, can you help me?

POLICEMAN **Hai. Nan deshō.**

Yes. What's the matter?

(nah-koo-shteh)

ANNE **Handobaggu o, nakushite**
(shee-mah-ee-mahsh-tah)
shimaimashita.

My purse is gone!

POLICEMAN **Dō shita no desu ka.**

What happened?

ANNE **Watakushi wa, shoppingu**
(yah) *(kehn-boo-tsoo)*
ya kenbutsu o shite imashita.
(doh-koh-kah) *(oh-kee-wah-soo-reh-teh)* *(kee-tah)*
Dokoka ni, okiwasurete kita
(chee-gah-ee)
ni chigai arimasen.

I've been shopping and sightseeing. I must have

left it somewhere.

(kee-chōh-heen)

POLICEMAN **Kichōhin wa.**

Any valuables?

ANNE **Hai. Pasupōto to,**
(koo-reh-jeet-toh) *(kāh-doh)* *(toh-rah-beh-rāh*
kurejitto kādo to, toraberā
chehk-koo) *(hah-eet-teh)*
chekku ga haitte imashita.
(dōh) *(shtah-rah)*
Dō shitara, ii deshō.

Yes. My passport, my credit cards, my traveler's

checks. What shall I do?

POLICEMAN **Saisho ni, namae o**

oshiete kudasai.

First, tell me your name.

ANNE **An Sumisu desu.**

Anne Smith.

(dehn-wah)

POLICEMAN **Watakushi ga denwa o**
(ah-ee-dah) *(choht-toh)*
suru aida, chotto matte
(sheen-pah-ee) *(shee-nah-koo-teh)*
kudasai. Shinpai shinakute

Please wait a moment while I make a phone call.

And don't worry. We'll find your purse.

ii desu yo. Handobaggu wa
(mee-tsoo-kah-ree-mahs)
mitsukarimasu.

(after five minutes)

(shee-rah-seh)
POLICEMAN   **Ii shirase desu.**
(dah-reh-kah)
Dareka ga anata no handobaggu
(toh-koo-nah-ee) *(koh-bahn)*
o, koko kara tōkunai   kōban
(toh-doh-keh-mahsh-tah)
ni todokemashita.

Good news. Someone turned in your purse at a

police substation not far from here.

(hohn-toh) *(tahs-KAH-ree-mahsh-tah)*
ANNE   **Hontō ni, tasukarimashita.**
(beek-koo-ree)
Soshite, bikkuri shimashita.

I'm so relieved. And surprised.

(foo-tsoo)
POLICEMAN   **Nihonjin wa futsū,**
(oh-toh-shee-moh-noh) *(toh-doh-keh-mahs)*
otoshimono o   todokemasu.

Japanese usually turn in lost items.

(nahn-teh) *(shoh-jee-kee)*
ANNE   **Nante   shōjiki na hitotachi**
(ee-tah-dah-ee-teh)
deshō. Tasukete itadaite,

hontō ni arigatō gozaimashita.

Such honest people! I'm very grateful for your

help.

Can you answer these questions based on the dialogue?

1. An san wa, nani o nakushite shimaimashita ka.

_____

2. Nihonjin wa, futsū otoshimono o todokemasu ka?

_____

| 8 | **(koo-roo-mah)**
Kuruma
Cars

(doh-roh)
Dōro de
On the road |

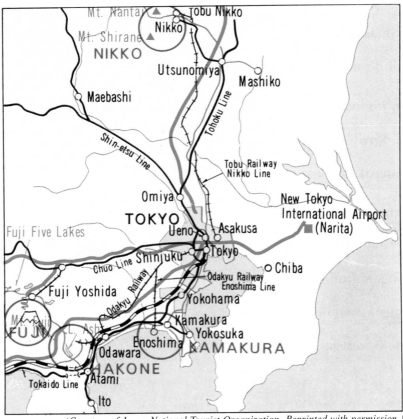

(Courtesy of Japan National Tourist Organization. Reprinted with permission.)

Driving in Japan isn't for the faint-hearted! The steering wheel is on the *right* side of the car, and you drive on the *left* side of the road. Most expressway signs are in Japanese. Non-express roads may be narrow and usually have no sidewalks. Speedometers are only in kilometers, streets are crowded with pedestrians, bicycles, vendors, and cars, and penalties for accidents are high.

(rehn-tah-kāh) **(eh-gyōh-shoh)**
RENTAKĀ NO EIGYŌSHO DE
At the Car Rental Agency

Mark is a brave, adventurous soul! He has decided to rent a car and take his family for an excursion into the Japanese countryside. They're going to start with the Great Buddha, or Daibutsu, in Kamakura, a seaside town not far from Tokyo.

MARK   **Ohayō gozaimasu. Kuruma**   Good morning. I'd like to rent a car.

o karitai no desu ga.

71

CLERK   Mochiron desu. Kikan *(kee-kahn)*
(doh-noh) (koo-rah-ee)
wa, dono   kurai desu ka.

Of course. For how long?

MARK   **Yaku isshūkan desu.**

About a week.

CLERK   **Sō desu nē.** *(neh)*   **Subaru to** *(soo-bah-roo)*
(toh-yoh-tah)
Toyota ga arimasu. Toyota
(hoh)   (oh-kee)
no hō ga, ōkii desu.

Let's see. We have a Subaru and a Toyota. The
Toyota is larger.

MARK   **Toyota o, kudasai.**
(ryoh-keen)   (kee-roh) (soo)
Ryōkin niwa, kiro   sū ga

fukumarete imasu ka.

I'll take the Toyota. Is the mileage included in the
price?

CLERK   **Hai, fukumarete imasu**
(gah-soh-reen) (dah-ee)   (oh-kyah-koo)
ga, gasorin   dai wa, okyaku
(sah-mah)   (oh-shee-hah-rah-ee)
sama ga oshiharai kudasai.
(kohk-sah-ee)   (mehn-kyoh-shoh)
Kokusai   menkyosho to

kurejitto kādo o, onegai

shimasu.

Yes, but you pay for the gas. May I have your
international driver's license and a credit card,
please?

MARK   **Gia no shifuto no shikata** *(gee-ah)   (shee-foo-toh)   (shkah-tah)*
(rah-ee-toh) (tskeh-kah-tah)
to, raito no tsukekata o
(moh-rah-eh-mahs)
oshiete moraemasu ka.

Can you show me how the gear shift and the
lights work?

CLERK   **Mochiron desu. Kagi to**
(shoh-roo-ee)
kuruma no shorui o dōzo.
(goh-ahn-nah-ee)
Kuruma made, goannai
(ee-tah-shee-mahs)
itashimasu.

Of course. Here are the keys and the car papers.
I'll come with you to the car.

Pretend that you want to rent a car. Can you fill in these lines from the dialogue?

1. Ohayō gozaimasu. K_____desu ga.

2. Kikan wa, dono kurai desu ka.

   Yaku_____.

3. Subaru to Toyota ga arimasu. Toyota no hō ga ōkii desu.

   T_____o_____.

(tah-ee-seh-tsoo) *(nah)* *(hyoh-gehn)*
Taisetsu na hyōgen
Some essential expressions

(mah-yoht-teh)
Michi ni, mayotte shimaimashita.   I'm lost.

(chee-kah-koo) *(shoo-ree)* *(koh-joh)*
Chikaku ni, shūri   kōjō ga arimasu ka.   Is there a garage nearby?

Nan deshō ka.   What's the matter?

(koh-noh-mah-mah)
Konomama, massugu ikimasu.   Continue straight ahead.

Koko de hidari ni magatte,   Turn left here, then right.

(soh-reh-kah-rah)
sorekara migi ni magarimasu.

(kohn-deh)
Michi ga, konde imasu.   There's a lot of traffic.

(tah-dah-shee)
Anata ga, tadashii desu.   You're right.

(yoh-koo) *(nah-ee)*
Anata ga, yoku   nai desu.   You're wrong.

kagi   keys

(mehn-kyoh) *(shoh)*
menkyo   sho   driver's license

(toh-roh-koo)
tōroku sho   registration (car papers)

gasorin   gasoline

(kee-tah)
kita   north

(mee-nah-mee)
minami   south

ANSWERS

Dialogue 1. Kuruma o karitai no desu ga. 2. Yaku isshūkan desu. 3. Toyota o kudasai.

(hee-gah-shee) **higashi**	east
(nee-shee) **nishi**	west
kado	corner
shingō	traffic light
(ah-kah) **aka shingō**	red light
(ah-oh) **ao shingō**	green light
(rahs-shoo) *(ah-wāh)* **rasshu awā**	rush hour
(hoh-kehn) **hoken**	insurance
(chōō-shah) **chūsha**	parking
(soh-koo-doh) *(seh-gehn)* **sokudo seigen**	speed limit
(ee-hahn) *(kehn)* **sokudo ihan no ken**	speeding ticket
(chee-zoo) **dōro chizu**	road map

Now match the Japanese with the English expression.

1. minami	a. parking
2. sokudo seigen	b. west
3. kagi	c. red light
4. dōro chizu	d. south
5. Nan deshō.	e. keys
6. chūsha	f. speed limit
7. rasshu awā	g. There's a lot of traffic.
8. kado	h. corner
9. menkyo sho	i. rush hour
10. Michi ga, konde imasu.	j. driver's license
11. aka shingō	k. road map
12. nishi	l. What's the matter?

DŌRO HYOSHIKI

Road Signs

If you're planning to drive while you're abroad, spend some time memorizing the meanings of these signs.

Emergency
Telephone

Caution

Stop

Slow Down

Minimum
Speed

No Parking over
60 Minutes

No Passing

Sound Horn

Parking

No Parking

No Parking,
No Standing

Standing
Permitted

Pedestrians
Only

Cars Only

Bicycles Only

Service Area

Detour

Exit

No Entrance

Entrance
to Expressway

Road Closed

National
Highway

No Right Turn

No U Turn

Traffic Island

Two Way Traffic
Dividing Line

One Way

This Lane for Motorcycles
and Lightweight Cars

GASORIN SUTANDO DE
(stahn-doh)

At the Service Station

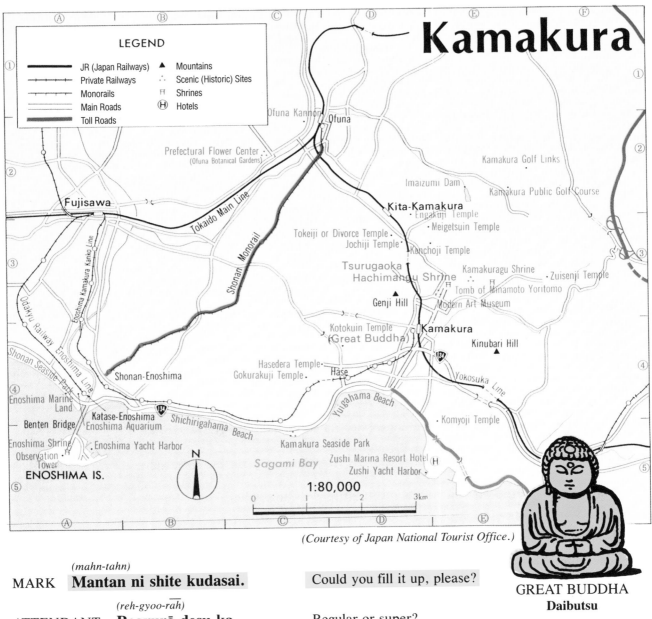

(Courtesy of Japan National Tourist Office.)

GREAT BUDDHA
Daibutsu

MARK	*(mahn-tahn)* **Mantan ni shite kudasai.**	Could you fill it up, please?
ATTENDANT	*(reh-gyoo-rāh)* **Regyurā desu ka,** *(hah-ee-oh-koo)* **haioku desu ka.**	Regular or super?
MARK	**Haioku o, onegai shimasu.** *(oh-ee-roo)* *(mee-zoo)* *(tah-ee-yah)* **Oiru to, mizu to, taiya no** *(kōo-kee)* *(ah-tsoo)* *(shee-rah-beh-teh)* **kūki atsu o shirabete** **moraemasu ka.**	Super, please. And could you check the oil and water and the tire pressure, please?

ATTENDANT *(soo-beh-teh)* **Subete daijōbu desu.** Everything is okay.

MARK *(dah-ee-boo-tsoo) (mee)* **Daibutsu o mi ni ikitai** *(ee-keh-bah)* **no desu ga. Dō ikeba ii** **desu ka.** We want to go to see the Daibutsu. How do we get there?

ATTENDANT *(kahn-tahn)* **Sore wa, kantan desu.** **Kono michi o konomama massugu** **itte, shingō de hidari ni** **magarimasu. Sugu,** *(soo-goo) (wah-kah-ree-mahs)* **wakarimasu** **yo.** It's easy. Continue straight on this road, and turn left at the traffic light. Then you can't miss it!

MARK **Michi wa, konde imasu ka.** Is there much traffic?

ATTENDANT *(ahn-mah-ree)* **Iie. Anmari konde** **imasen. Daibutsu o** **otanoshimi kudasai.** No, not much at all. Enjoy the Daibutsu.

Now write these important words and phrases from the dialogue:

1. Could you fill it up, please? _____

2. Could you check the oil and water and the tire pressure, please? _____

_____

3. Everything is okay. _____

4. How do we get there? _____

5. Turn left at the traffic light. _____

_____

KURUMA
The Car

(wah-ee-pāh)
waipā
windshield wipers

(dahs-shoo-bōh-doh)
dasshubōdo
dashboard

(shee-foo-toh) (reh-bāh)
shifuto rebā
gear shift stick

(ahk-seh-roo)
akuseru
accelerator

(boo-rēh-kee)
burēki
brake pedal

(koo-raht-chee)
kuratchi
clutch pedal

(kēh-teh-kee)
keiteki
horn

(hahn-doh-roo)
handoru
steering wheel

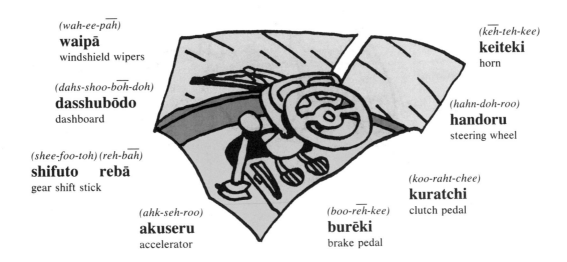

(foo-rohn-toh) (gah-rah-soo)
furonto garasu
windshield

(ehn-jeen)
enjin
motor

(rah-jee-ēh-tāh)
rajiētā
radiator

(bohn-neht-toh)
bonnetto
hood

(baht-teh-rēē)
batterī
battery

(hehd-doh-rah-ee-toh)
heddoraito
headlights

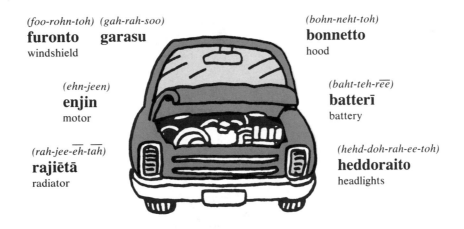

(toh-rahn-koo)
toranku
trunk

(bahk-koo   rah-ee-toh)
bakku raito
backup light

(hōh-kōh) (shee-jee-tōh)
hōkō shijitō
directional signal

(boo-rēh-kee) (rah-ee-toh)
burēki raito
brake light

(oo-shee-roh noh mah-doh gah-rah-soo)
ushiro no mado garasu
rear window

(tēh-roo) (rahn-poo)
tēru ranpu
rear light

(nahn-bāh   poo-rēh-toh)
nanbā purēto
license plate

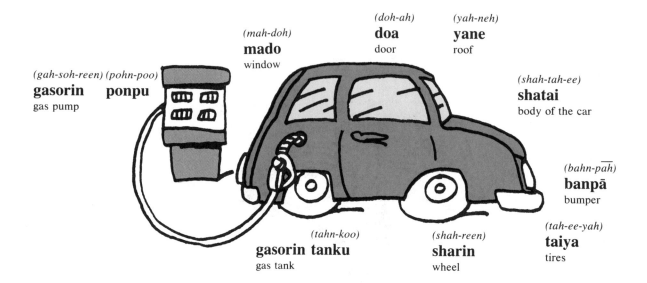

(gah-soh-reen) (pohn-poo)
gasorin ponpu
gas pump

(mah-doh)
mado
window

(doh-ah)
doa
door

(yah-neh)
yane
roof

(shah-tah-ee)
shatai
body of the car

(bahn-pah̄)
banpā
bumper

(tahn-koo)
gasorin tanku
gas tank

(shah-reen)
sharin
wheel

(tah-ee-yah)
taiya
tires

Now fill in the names for the following auto parts.

Komatta toki ni yakudatsu kotoba

(koh-maht-tah) *(toh-kee)* *(yah-koo-dah-tsoo)*

Some useful phrases in case of problems

Tasukete moraemasu ka.
Can you help me?

(pahn-koo)
Panku desu.
I have a flat tire.

(oo-goh-kee-mah-sehn)
Kuruma ga, ugokimasen.
My car has broken down.

(kah-kah-ree-mah-sehn)
Enjin ga, kakarimasen.
My car won't start.

(gah-soo) *(keh-tsoo)*
Gasu   ketsu desu.
I've run out of gas.

(kee-kee-mah-sehn)
Burēki ga kikimasen.
My brakes don't work.

(oh-bah-hee-toh)
Ōbāhīto shite imasu.
My car is overheating.

(kehn-een) *(shah)*
Kenin   sha ga, hitsuyō desu.
I need a tow truck.

(moht-teh)
Rajiētā ga, motte imasu.
The radiator is leaking.

(toh-rahn-soo-mees-shohn) *(koh-wah-reh-teh)*
Toransumisshon ga, kowarete
The transmission is

shimaimashita.
broken.

(ah-gaht-teh)
Batterī ga, agatte shimaimashita.
The battery is dead.

Hōkō shiji no raito ga,
The signal lights don't

(tskee-mah-sehn)
tsukimasen.
work.

Oiru ga, motte imasu.
The oil is leaking.

(eh-ah-kohn) *(hee-tah)*
Eakon   (hītā) ga, kikimasen.
The air conditioning

(heater) doesn't work.

Fill in the blanks by referring to the new expressions.

1. Kuruma ga _____ .
   <u>has broken down</u>

2. _____ ga kikimasen.
   <u>the brakes</u>

ANSWERS

Fill in blanks 1. ugokimasen 2. Burēki

81

3. Batterī ga _____ .

                   is dead

4. Oiru ga _____ .

                 is leaking

5. _____ ga kikimasen.

   the air conditioning

(mēh-rēh)   (hōh)

Meirei hō
The Imperative

You've already learned several ways to ask for things in Japanese. Now let's look at another way, the imperative, or command form of the verb.

Remember that with imperative verbs, the subject is "YOU" (understood), so you don't use a pronoun.

To form the imperative in Japanese, first take the present continuous form of the verb, the **-te** form:

         hanashite imasu   am speaking

Then drop the **imasu**, and replace it with **kudasai**:

       hanashite kudasai   please speak

       (yook-koo-ree)
       Yukkuri hanashite kudasai.   Please speak slowly.
       Kite kudasai.   Please come.
       Kiite kudasai.   Please listen.
       Tasukete kudasai.   Please help me.

The negative is more complex. The guidelines here will work for many, *but not all*, verbs.

Start with the infinitive. If it ends in **-eru** or **-iru**, drop the **ru**. Then add **-naide**.

        oshieru   explain

(oh-shee-ee-nah-ee-deh)
Oshienaide kudasai.   Please don't explain it.

For other infinitives, drop the **final vowel** and add **-anaide.**

        iku   go

ANSWERS

Fill in blanks 3. agatte shimaimashita **4.** motte imasu **5.** Eakon

82

(ee-kah-nah-ee-deh)
Ikanaide kudasai. Please don't go.

Suru (do) and **kuru** (come) are irregular.

(shee-nah-ee-deh)
Shinaide kudasai. Please don't do it.

(koh-nah-ee-deh)
Konaide kudasai. Please don't come.

Another form of the imperative uses "let's"—"Let's go," "Let's eat," "Let's buy it."

(mah-shoh)
First take the present form of the verb. Remove the **-masu**, and replace it with **-mashō**.

It looks like this:

ikimasu	go	**Ikimashō.**	Let's go!
kaimasu	buy	*(reen-goh)* **Ringo o kaimashō.**	Let's buy an apple.
tabemasu	eat	*(ah-sah) (goh-hahn)* **Asa gohan o tabemashō.**	Let's eat breakfast.

To form a question, "Shall we" in English, just add **ka** at the end:

Tabemashō ka. Shall we eat?

Now try a few yourself!

1. Kamakura e _____ . (Let's go)

2. Ringo o _____ . (Let's eat)

3. Daibutsu o _____ . (Shall we see)

4. Keikan ni _____ . (Let's ask)

5. Eigo o _____ . (Let's speak)

83

Dōshi o mō sukoshi
More verbs

	(moh-tsoo) **MOTSU** to have, to own, to possess		
Note: This verb is used mainly in the present and past continuous forms			
		AFFIRMATIVE	NEGATIVE
PRESENT CONTINUOUS		**motte imasu**	**motte imasen**
PAST CONTINUOUS		**motte imashita**	**motte imasen deshita**

	(koo-roo) **KURU** to come	
	AFFIRMATIVE	NEGATIVE
	(kee-mahs)	*(kee-mah-sehn)*
PRESENT	**kimasu**	**kimasen**
PRESENT CONTINUOUS	**kite imasu**	**kite imasen**
PAST	**kimashita**	**kimasen deshita**

(deh-kee-mahs)　　　　*(nah-keh-reh-bah*　　*nah-ree-mah-sehn)*

Dekimasu to nakereba narimasen
Can and Must

To express **can** or **can do** in Japanese, use **dekimasu**. Here's how:

	(deh-kee-roo) **DEKIRU** to be able, can		
		(deh-kee-mah-sehn)	
dekimasu	can	**dekimasen**	can't
(deh-kee-mahsh-tah)			
dekimashita	could	**dekimasen deshita**	couldn't

You can use **dekimasu** with nouns. In this case, it means "is possible."

Nihongo ga **dekimasu.**	I can speak Japanese.
(teh-nees)	
Tenisu ga **dekimasu.**	I can play tennis.

Notice that in these sentences, the verbs "speak" and "play" aren't needed. **Dekimasu** is used alone. The literal meanings become "Japanese is possible (for me)," and "Tennis is possible (for me)."

With verbs, it's different. Start with the infinitive form of the verb (**kuru, iku, hanasu**), then use **koto ga**, followed by the appropriate form of **dekiru**.

Kuru koto ga dekimasu.	I can come.
Iku koto ga dekimasen.	I can't go.
Oshieru koto ga dekimasu ka.	Can you explain?

To express **have to** or **must** in English is easy. In Japanese it's more complicated. The explanation here *won't* work for *all* verbs, but it will help you to get started.

Begin with the infinitive of the verb.

(nah-keh-reh-bah) (nah-ree-mah-sehn)

If the infinitive ends in **-eru** or **-iru**, drop the **ru**. Then add **-nakereba   narimasen.**

oshieru   explain   **oshienakereba narimasen**   must explain

For other infinitives, drop the **final vowel** and add **-a**. Then add **-nakereba narimasen.**

hanasu   speak   **hanasanakereba narimasen**   must speak

Kuru and **suru** are irregular.

kuru	**konakereba narimasen**	must come
suru	**shinakereba narimasen**	must do

For the negative, start with the **-te** form (the first word of the present continuous form of the verb). Then add **wa narimasen.**

Kite wa narimasen.   I mustn't come.
Ano hito wa **itte wa narimasen.**   He shouldn't go.

Can you supply the missing Japanese?

1. Iku _____ .
   I can go.

2. Eigo _____ .
   Can you speak English?

3. Oshienakereba _____ .
   I must explain.

4. Utau _____ .
   I can't sing.

5. Kuru _____ .
   He can come.

ANSWERS

Missing words 1. Iku koto ga dekimasu. 2. Eigo ga dekimasu ka. 3. Oshienakereba narimasen. 4. Utau koto ga dekimasen. 5. Kuru koto ga dekimasu.

(heets-yōh)   *(heen)*
HITSUYŌ HIN
Essentials

(eh-āh maht-toh-rehs)
eā mattoresu
air mattress

(yōh-fkoo)
yōfuku
clothes

(kahn-zoo-meh)
kanzume
cans

(kah-ee)
kai
paddles

(mōh-foo)
mōfu
blanket

(tehn-toh)
tento
tent

ki
tree

(tah-ee-yōh)
taiyō
sun

(oh-gah-wah)
ogawa
brook

(soo-rēē-peen-goo bahg-goo)
surīpingu baggu
sleeping bag

(kah-ee-chōō dehn-toh)
kaichū dentō
flashlight

(bahs-keht-toh)
basuketto
basket

(hah-koh)
hako
box

(kah-nōō)
kanū
canoe

(bah-keh-tsoo)
baketsu
bucket

(tsoo-ree-zah-oh)
tsurizao
rod

(tsoo-ree)
tsuri
fishing

(sehn-noo-kee)
sennuki
corkscrew

(ryōō-ree yōh-goo)
ryōri yōgu
cooking utensils

(bōō-tsoo)
būtsu
boots

(sehn-mehn)
senmen yōgu
toilet articles

(mah-hōh been)
mahō bin
thermos

(kēh-tah-ee rah-jee-oh)
keitai rajio
portable radio

(maht-chee)
matchi
matches

The Japanese countryside is spectacular with its beautiful mountains, forests, lakes, and rivers—a paradise for people who enjoy camping. Campsites are plentiful and inexpensive. They can be crowded during July and August, so reservations are advised for those months.

KYANPU JŌ E
(joh)
To the Campsite

Now read the following dialogues, which contain some useful words, expressions, and information on camping. Read them aloud, repeating each line several times so you know how to pronounce the new words.

MARK   **Sumimasen ga. Chikaku ni,**

kyanpu jō ga arimasu ka.

Excuse me. Is there a campsite nearby?

FARMER   **Hai. Koko kara yaku**
(nee-jook-kee-roh)   *(hyoh-shee-kee)*
nijukkiro desu. Hyōshiki ni
(shee-tah-gaht-teh)
shitagatte, itte kudasai.

Yes. About 20 kilometers from here. Just follow those signs.

MARK   **Soko niwa, basurūmu ga**
(noh-mee-mee-zoo)
arimasu ka. Nomimizu mo

arimasu ka.

Are there any bathrooms there? And drinking water?

FARMER   *(keet-toh)*
Kitto arimasu. Kyanpu
(koo-reh-mahs)
jō de, oshiete kuremasu.

I'm sure there are. They can tell you at the campsite.

KYANPU JŌ DE
(kyahn-poo) (joh)
At the Campsite

MARK   *(toh-mah-reh-roo) (bah-shoh)*
Tomareru   basho ga arimasu

ka.

Do you have room for us?

DIRECTOR   **Hai. Dono kurai taizai**
(tah-ee-zah-ee)
suru yotei desu ka.
(yoh-teh)

Yes. How long are you planning to stay?

MARK   *(foo-tah) (bahn)   (mee)*
Futa   ban ka, mi ban desu.

Shawā ga arimasu ka.

Two or three nights. Are there any showers?

DIRECTOR	**Shawā wa arimasen ga,**	No showers, but we do have a public bath house.
	(tah-ee-shoo) *(yoh-koo-joh)* *(shee-seh-tsoo)*	
	taishū yokujō no shisetsu ga	
	arimasu.	
	(kohn-yoh-koo)	
ANNE	**Konyoku desu ka.**	Men and women together?
	(sheen-pah-ee)	
DIRECTOR	**Shinpai shinakute ii**	Don't worry. There are separate facilities for men
	(dahn-joh) *(beh-tsoo-beh-tsoo)*	and women.
	desu yo. Danjo betsubetsu	
	desu.	
	(moo-ryoh)	
MARK	**Muryō desu ka.**	Is it free?
DIRECTOR	**Iie. Yon hyaku gojū**	No. It costs 450 yen.
	en desu.	
MARK	**Nomimizu wa dō desu ka.**	What about drinking water?
DIRECTOR	**Mochiron. Koko niwa,**	Of course. We have good water here.
	ii mizu ga arimasu.	
MARK	**Watakushitachi no basho**	How much will our site cost?
	wa, ikura desu ka.	
	(kah-ree-tah-ee)	
DIRECTOR	**Tento o karitai**	Do you want to rent a tent?
	desu ka.	
MARK	**Iie, jibun no o motte**	No, we have our own.
	imasu.	
	(soh-reh-deh-wah) *(hee-toh)*	
DIRECTOR	**Soredewa, kazoku hito**	Then it's just 500 yen per night for your family.
	(bahn) *(tsoo-kee)*	
	ban ni tsuki go hyaku en desu.	
	(yah-soo-ee) *(neh)*	
MARK	**Yasui desu ne!**	That's cheap!

Match these Japanese expressions with their English equivalents:

1. basuketto		a. cooking utensils	
2. kanzume		b. flashlight	
3. mōfu		c. sleeping bag	
4. senmen yōgu		d. tent	
5. matchi		e. matches	
6. tento		f. blanket	
7. tsuri		g. fishing	
8. surīpingu baggu		h. toilet articles	
9. kaichū dentō		i. cans	
10. ryōri yōgu		j. basket	

(shoh-koo-ryōh-heen tehn)

SHOKURYŌHIN TEN DE

At the Grocery Store

(nah-nee-kah)

CLERK **Irasshaimase. Nanika,**
(goh-ee-ree-yōh)
goiriyō desu ka.

Welcome. May I help you?

(oh-koh-meh) (eek-kee-roo)

MARY **Hai. Okome o ikkiro to,**
(oh-sah-keh)   (hah-roo)   (yoh)
osake o ippon to, hamu o yo
(kee-reh) (ryōh-ree)   (ah-boo-rah)
kire to, ryōri yō no abura o
(reet-toh-roo)
ichi rittoru hoshii no desu ga.

Yes. I'd like a kilo of rice, a bottle of sake, four slices of ham, and a liter of cooking oil.

CLERK **Kyanpu jō ni, otomari**

desu ka.

Are you staying at the campsite?

MARK **Hai, sō desu.**

Yes, we are.

(ah-meh-ree-kah-jeen)

CLERK **Amerikajin desu ka.**

Are you Americans?

ANSWERS

Matching 1. j 2. i 3. f 4. h 5. e 6. d 7. g 8. c 9. b 10. a

89

MARK   **Hai. Watakushitachi wa,**   Yes. This is our first time here.

           koko wa hajimete desu.

           (nah-roo-hoh-doh) *(hoh-kah)*
CLERK   **Naruhodo.**   **Hoka ni**   I see. Will there be anything else?

           nanika, goiriyō desu ka.

           (dah-keh)
MARY   **Iie. Sore dake da to**   No. I think that's it.
(oh-moh-ee-mahs)
           omoimasu.

           (chōh-dah-ee)
CLERK   **Ni sen en, chōdai shimasu.**   That will be 2000 yen.

MARY   **Hai, dōzo.**   Here you are.

CLERK   **Arigatō gozaimasu. Sayōnara.**   Thank you. Goodbye.

What is the Japanese for these expressions?

1. a kilo of rice _____

2. a bottle of sake _____

3. a liter of cooking oil _____

90

Dōshi o mō sukoshi

(doh-shee) (oh) (moh) (skoh-shee)

More Verbs

You will need to know how to say "know" and "understand" in Japanese.

	(shee-roo) **SHIRU** to know	
	AFFIRMATIVE	NEGATIVE
PRESENT	*(shee-ree-mahs)* **shirimasu**	*(shee-ree-mah-sehn)* **shirimasen**
PRESENT CONTINUOUS	*(sheet-teh)* **shitte imasu**	**shitte imasen**
PAST	*(shee-ree-mahsh-tah)* **shirimashita**	**shirimasen deshita**

	(wah-kah-roo) **WAKARU** to understand	
	AFFIRMATIVE	NEGATIVE
PRESENT	*(wah-kah-ree-mahs)* **wakarimasu**	*(wah-kah-ree-mah-sehn)* **wakarimasen**
PRESENT CONTINUOUS	*(wah-kaht-teh)* **wakatte imasu**	**wakatte imasen**
PAST	*(wah-kah-ree-mahsh-tah)* **wakarimashita**	**wakarimasen deshita**

If you go camping, you'll certainly need the next verb!

	(ah-roo-koo) **ARUKU** to walk	
	AFFIRMATIVE	NEGATIVE
PRESENT	*(ah-roo-kee-mahs)* **arukimasu**	*(ah-roo-kee-mah-sehn)* **arukimasen**
PRESENT CONTINUOUS	*(ah-roo-ee-teh)* **aruite imasu**	**aruite imasen**
PAST	*(ah-roo-kee-mahsh-tah)* **arukimashita**	**aruite imashita**

Dō iimasu ka

(dōh) *(ēe-mahs)* *(kah)*

How do you say . . .

Here are some everyday expressions that might come in handy on your camping excursion.

(ah-tsoo-ee)
Karera wa, atsui desu.
They are hot.

(koh-wah-gaht-teh)
Otoko no ko tachi wa, kowagatte imasu.
The boys are afraid.

(oh-nah-kah) *(soo-ee-teh)*
Inu wa, onaka ga suite imasu.
The dog is hungry.

(sah-moo-ee)
Watakushitachi wa, samui desu.
We are cold.

(koh-maht-teh)
Onna no hito wa, komatte imasu.
The woman is embarrassed.

(neh-moo-ee)
Otoko no hito wa, nemui desu.
The man is sleepy.

Can you fill in the missing Japanese words?

1. Onna no hito wa _____ .
   is embarrassed

2. Inu wa _____ .
   is hungry

3. Otoko no hito wa, _____ .
   is sleepy

4. Otoko no ko tachi wa _____ .
   are afraid

5. Watakushitachi wa _____ .
   are cold

1.   2.   3.

4.   5.

ANSWERS

Fill in words 1. komatte imasu 2. onaka ga suite imasu 3. nemui desu 4. kowagatte imasu 5. samui desu

92

10

(tehn-kee) *(kee-seh-tsoo)*
Tenki, kisetsu
The weather, the seasons

(tsoo-kee) *(hee-nee-chee)*
Tsuki, hinichi
Months and days

ichi gatsu

ni gatsu

san gatsu

shi gatsu

go gatsu

roku gatsu

shichi gatsu

hachi gatsu

ku gatsu

jū gatsu

jūichi gatsu

jūni gatsu

(gah-tsoo)

ichi gatsu
January

ni gatsu
February

san gatsu
March

shi gatsu
April

go gatsu
May

roku gatsu
June

shichi gatsu
July

hachi gatsu
August

ku gatsu
September

jū gatsu
October

jūichi gatsu
November

jūni gatsu
December

93

TENKI WA DŌ DESU KA
How is the Weather?

(foo-yoo)
Fuyu desu.   It's winter.

Samui desu.   It's cold.

Totemo samui desu.   It's very cold.
(yoo-kee)   (foot-teh)
Yuki ga futte imasu.   It's snowing.

(hah-roo)
Haru desu.   It's spring.
(ah-tah-tah-kah-ee)
Atatakai desu.   It's warm.
(hee)   (teht-teh)
Hi ga tette imasu.   It's sunny.

(nah-tsoo)
Natsu desu.   It's summer.

Atsui desu.   It's hot.
(sheek-keh)   (tah-kah-ee)
Shikke ga takai desu.   It's humid.
(moo-shee-ah-tsoo-ee)
Mushiatsui desu.   It's hot and humid.

Ii tenki desu.   It's a beautiful day.
(ah-meh)
Ame ga futte imasu.   It's raining.
(ah-rah-shee)
Arashi desu.   It's stormy.
(kah-mee-nah-ree)   (naht-teh)   (ee-nah-zoo-mah)
Kaminari ga natte   inazuma   It's thundering and lightning.
     (hee-kaht-teh)
     ga hikkate imasu.

(ah-kee)
Aki desu.   It's fall.
(soo-zoo-shēē)
Suzushii desu.   It's cool.
(kee-ree)
Kiri desu.   It's foggy.
       (hah-geh-shee-koo)
Ame ga hageshiku futte   It's raining heavily.

     imasu.

Tenki ga ii desu.
(wah-roo-ee)
Tenki ga warui desu.

The weather is beautiful.

The weather is awful.

Can you describe the weather in the pictures below?

1. _____

2. _____

3. _____

4. _____

5. _____

6. _____

(ah-kah-roo-ee)
akarui
light

(ah-sah)
asa
morning

(hee-roo-mah)
hiruma
day

gogo
afternoon

(yōo-gah-tah)
yūgata
evening

(koo-rah-ee)
kurai
dark

(yoh-roo)
yoru
night

(yoh-bee)
YŌBI
Days of the Week

Do you remember the days of the week in Japanese? If not, here's a brief review:

getsu yōbi
Monday

ka yōbi
Tuesday

sui yōbi
Wednesday

moku yōbi
Thursday

kin yōbi
Friday

do yōbi
Saturday

nichi yōbi
Sunday

HINICHI
Days of the Month

For the days of the month—you guessed it! Another set of numbers to learn. Here they are:

	(tsoo-ee-tah-chee)			*(moo-ee-kah)*			*(joo-ee-chee nee-chee)*
1st	**tsuitachi**	6th	**muika**	11th	**jūichi nichi**		
	(foots-kah)		*(nah-noh-kah)*		*(joo-nee nee-chee)*		
2nd	**futsuka**	7th	**nanoka**	12th	**jūni nichi**		
	(meek-kah)		*(yoh-kah)*		*(joo-yohk-kah)*		
3rd	**mikka**	8th	**yōka**	14th	**jūyokka**		
	(yohk-kah)		*(koh-koh-noh-kah)*		*(hah-tsoo-kah)*		
4th	**yokka**	9th	**kokonoka**	20th	**hatsuka**		
	(ee-tsoo-kah)		*(toh-kah)*		*(nee-joo-yohk-kah)*		
5th	**itsuka**	10th	**tōka**	24th	**nijūyokka**		

For days not on this list, use the cardinal numbers you have learned, and add **-nichi** at the end (as in 11th and 12th above). For example, the 30th of the month would be **san jū nichi**.

Now fill in the following dates in Japanese.

1. January 1 _____

2. February 17 _____

3. May 8 _____

4. June 12 _____

5. August 14 _____

ANSWERS

Dates 1. ichi gatsu tsuitachi **2.** ni gatsu jūshichi nichi **3.** go gatsu yōka **4.** roku gatsu jūni nichi **5.** hachi gatsu jūyokka

The Smith family is staying in a hotel. Mary and her daughter, Anne, are sharing a room.   It's early morning.

MARY   **Ohayō gozaimasu.**   Good morning.

ANNE   **Nanji desu ka.**   What time is it?

MARY   **Shichi ji han desu.**   7:30.

        (sohn-nah)   *(dohn-nah)*

ANNE   **Mō sonna jikan. Donna**   Already? What's the weather like?

      tenki desu ka.

      (soo-bah-rah-shee)

MARY   **Subarashii desu.**   Magnificent. What a sunrise!

      (oo-tsoo-koo-shee) *(hee-noh-deh)*

      Utsukushii   hinode yo.

        (yoh-hoh)

ANNE   **Donna tenki yohō desu ka.**   What's the weather forecast?

      (ah-tah-tah-kahk-teh)

MARY   **Atatakakute ii tenki**   Beautiful, mild weather. Temperature between 18

      (kee-ohn) *(sehs-shee)*

      desu. Kion wa, sesshi   and 20 degrees centigrade. This evening, overcast

      (doh)

      jūhachi do to nijū do no   with temperatures falling.

      (kohn-bahn)

      aida desu. Konban wa

      (koo-moh-ree) *(sah-gah-ree-mahs)*

      kumori de, kion ga sagarimasu.

      (oh-kee-mah-shoh)

ANNE   **Okimashō. Onaka ga,**   Let's get up. I'm hungry.

      suite imasu.

Try to complete the missing dialogue parts.

1. Ohayō g _____ .   Good morning.

2. N _____ ?   What time is it?

3. Donna t _____ d _____ ?   What's the weather like?

4. S_____ d _____ .   Magnificent.

ANSWERS

Dialogue 1. Ohayō gozaimasu. **2.** Nanji desu ka. **3.** Donna tenki desu ka. **4.** Subarashii desu.

(keh-yoh-shee)

KEIYŌSHI

Adjectives

Adjectives in Japanese come before the noun, as in English. One exception is adjectives of number, which follow the noun. Here are some common Japanese adjectives:

(oo-reh-shee)
ureshii
happy, glad

(kee-reh)
kirei
pretty

(oh-kee)
ōkii
big

(chee-sah-ee)
chiisai
small

(shee-zoo-kah)
shizuka
quiet

(yah-kah-mah-shee)
yakamashii
noisy

(oh-ee-shee)
oishii
delicious

ii
good, nice

(tah-kah-ee)
takai
expensive

(yah-soo-ee)
yasui
inexpensive, cheap

Japanese adjectives fall into two groups: they're sometimes called **-i** adjectives and **na** adjectives.

> **-i** adjective

a small child

chiisai kodomo

> **na** adjective

a beautiful woman

kirei na onna no hito

oishii gohan	delicious rice
ōkii heya	big room

But they conjugate, or change form, before the "to be" verb, **desu**, except in the present tense, which stays the same in the affirmative.

Gohan wa, **oishii** desu.	The rice is delicious.
Heya wa, **ōkii** desu.	The room is big.

To form the negative, drop the **-i** and add **-kunai**.

Gohan wa, **oishikunai** desu.	The rice isn't delicious.
Heya wa, **ōkikunai** desu.	The room isn't big.

To form the past, drop the **-i** and add **-katta**.

Gohan wa, **oishikatta** desu.	The rice was delicious.
Heya wa, **ōkikatta** desu.	The room was big.

To form the negative past, drop the **-i** and add **-kunakatta**.

Gohan wa, **oishikunakatta** desu.	The rice wasn't delicious.
Heya wa, **ōkikunakatta** desu.	The room wasn't big.

Note: **Ii** (good, nice) is an exception. The negative is **yokunai** desu. The past is **yokatta** desu. The negative past is **yokunakatta** desu.

na adjectives are different. They're used with **na** before a noun.

kirei na uchi	pretty house
shizuka na heya	quiet room

Before the verb "to be" they don't conjugate, or change form. Just add the appropriate form of **desu** at the end.

Uchi wa, **kirei** desu.	The house is pretty.
Heya wa, **shizuka** dewa arimasen.	The room isn't quiet.

For the past, use **deshita** as usual.

Uchi wa, **kirei** deshita.	The house was pretty.
Heya wa, **shizuka** dewa arimasen deshita.	The room wasn't quiet.

Following are some **na** adjectives. Refer to this list until they're familiar to you.

shizuka   quiet   **kirei** pretty   **jōzu** good at

heta   poor at   **suki** like, fond of   **kirai** dislike, not fond of
(yōo-meh)
yūmei famous

The following example will show you how to use a **-na** adjective before a noun and before a verb.

Tanaka san speaks good English.
Tanaka san wa **jōzu na** Eigo o hanashimasu.

As for Tanaka san, his English is good.
Tanaka san wa Eigo ga **jōzu desu.**

Here are some more examples.

I like this book.   Watakushi wa kono hon ga **suki** desu.

the book I like   **suki na** hon

This is the book I like.   Kore ga, watakushi ga **suki na** hon desu.

Now try some phrases and sentences with adjectives.

1. a nice man _____

2. a man that I like _____

3. an inexpensive book _____

4. a quiet room _____

5. good English _____

6. Mark is happy. _____ .

7. Mary is famous. _____ .

8. She speaks good Japanese. _____ .

11 | Hikōki no ryokō
(ryoh-kōh)

Plane trips

Kankō kenbutsu
(Kahn-kōh   kehn-boo-tsoo)

Sightseeing

A plane trip within Japan is an easy and enjoyable way to travel. In the Tokyo area, **Narita International Airport** is used for international flights, and **Haneda Airport** is used for domestic flights.

Here's some useful vocabulary. Try to find the items in the picture.

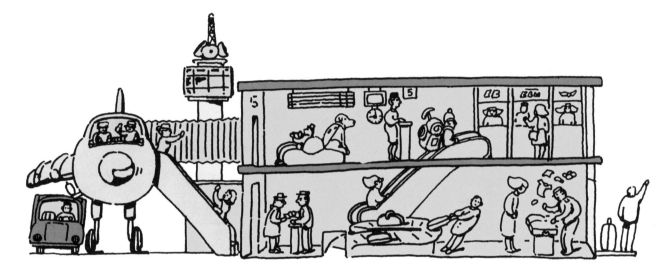

(kōh-kōo) *(gah-ee-shah)*
kōkū gaisha
airline

(zeh-kahn)
zeikan no kakariin
customs officer

(soh-jōo-shee) *(foo-koo)*
sōjūshi   fuku sōjūshi
pilot,   copilot

(keep-poo-oo-ree-bah)/
(chee-keht-toh kah-oon-tāh)
kippu uriba/chiketto kauntā
ticket counter

(ee-meen/(nyoo-kohk teh-tsoo-zoo-kee)
imin/nyūkoku tetsuzuki
immigration

(soo-choo-WĀH-dehs)
suchuwādesu
stewardess

(soo-choo-WĀH-doh)
suchuwādo
steward

(toh-kēh)
tokei
clock

(gēh-toh)
gēto
gate

(kahn-seh) *(tōh)*
kansei tō
control tower

(ehs-kah-rēh-tāh)
esukarētā
escalator

(nee-moh-tsoo)
nimotsu
luggage

(toh-rahk-koo)
torakku
truck

(oo-KEH-toh-ree-joh)
nimotsu uketorijo
baggage claim

HIKŌKI
(hee-kōh-kee)

The Plane

(hee-jōh-goo-chee)
hijōguchi
emergency exit

(toh-jōh-een)
tōjōin
crew

(mah-doh)
mado
window

(tsōō-roh)
tsūro
aisle

(kyah-koo-shtsoo)
kyakushitsu
cabin

(ree-ree-koo)
ririku
takeoff

(oh-bohn)
obon
tray

seki
seat

(kahs-sōh-roh)
kassōro
runway

(chah-koo-ree-koo)
chakuriku
landing

(shēē-toh)
shīto
seat belt

(beh-roo-toh)
beruto

(jōh-kyah-koo)
jōkyaku
passenger

There are certain words and expressions in this dialogue that you might hear or need on a plane. Read each line out loud.

STEWARDESS *(toh-jōh-kehn)* **Tōjōken o onegai shimasu.** Your boarding passes, please.

MARK **Hai, dōzo.** Here they are.

STEWARDESS *(oh-seh-kee)* *(soh-chee-rah)* **Oseki wa sochira de gozaimasu.** Your seats are right over there.

MARK **Arigatō.** Thank you.

STEWARDESS *(hohn-jee-tsoo)* **Honjitsu wa, Fuji** Thank you very much for using Fuji

102

(koh-koo) (been)
Kōkū san byaku ichi bin
(kah-nah-zah-wah) (goh-ree-yoh)
Kanazawa yuki o goriyō

itadaki, arigatō gozaimasu.
(mah-moh-nah-koo)
Mamonaku ririku itashimasu.
(shee-meh)
Shīto beruto o shime, kinen
(sah-een) (kee-eh-roo)
no sain ga kieru made,
(tah-bah-koh) (goh-ehn-ryoh)
tabako o goenryo kudasai.

Airways flight 301 to Kanazawa. We will take off

in a few minutes. Please fasten your seat belts

and observe the no smoking sign.

PILOT   **Ohayō gozaimasu.**
(koh-doh)
Honjitsu wa kōdo hassen
(meh-toh-roo) (hee-koh)
metoru de hikō itashimasu.
(shoh-goh)
Kanazawa niwa, shōgo ni

tōchaku no yotei desu.
(hah-reh)
Kanazawa no tenki wa hare,

kion wa sesshi jūgo do desu.

Hikō o, otanoshimi kudasai.

Good morning. We will be flying at an altitude of

8,000 meters. We will arrive in Kanazawa at

noon. The weather there is sunny, and the

temperature is 15 degrees celsius. Enjoy your

flight.

MARK   **Sumimasen ga. Kono bin**
(shoh-koo-jee) (deh-mahs)
dewa, shokuji ga demasu ka.

Excuse me, miss. Do you serve a meal on this

flight?

STEWARDESS   **Iie, demasen.**
(joo-soo)
Keredomo, jūsu, ocha,
(soo-nahk-koo)
sunakku ga gozaimasu.

No, we don't. But we'll serve some juice, tea,

and a light snack soon.

MARK   **Naruhodo. Makura to**

mōfu o onegai shimasu.

I see. May I have a pillow and blanket, please?

(kahsh-koh-mah-ree-mahsh-tah)
STEWARDESS   **Kashikomarimashita.**

Hai, dōzo.

Certainly. Here you are.

Can you give the Japanese equivalents for these expressions?

1. Your boarding pass, please. _____ .

2. Enjoy your flight. _____ .

3. Excuse me, miss/sir. _____ .

4. May I have a pillow and blanket, please. _____ .

5. Here you are. _____ .

Teinei na kotoba
Polite language

As you read the previous dialogue and others like it, you may have noticed that people in a service capacity—clerks, flight attendants, waitresses—use a different kind of language from that of the people they're serving. Let's look at a few lines from the airplane dialogue:

STEWARDESS **Oseki wa, sochira**   Your seats are right over there.

de gozaimasu.

This kind of language is different from the kind you're learning to speak. Take the word **oseki** (chair), for example. The **o** at the beginning makes it extra polite. And the verb **de gozaimasu** is extra polite too. For the all-purpose polite level *you* are learning to speak here, you would use the **desu** form of the verb.

As you know, Japanese has many politeness levels, and the rules governing their use take a while to learn. You don't need to be concerned about this for now. Just be aware that as you proceed in your study of Japanese you'll begin to notice the differences more and more. As a learner and a tourist, you aren't expected to use the extra-polite, or "**gozaimasu**" kind of language. But you do want to understand it when others use it!

(doh-shee   oh moh   skoh-shee)
Dōshi o mō sukoshi
More verbs

(oh-moh-oo) **OMOU** to think, to believe, to feel		
	AFFIRMATIVE	NEGATIVE
		(oh-moh-ee-mah-sehn)
PRESENT	omoimasu	omoimasen
	(oh-moht-teh)	
PRESENT CONTINUOUS	omotte imasu	omotte imasen
	(oh-moh-ee-mahsh-tah)	
PAST	omoimashita	omoimasen deshita

(tah-noh-moo) **TANOMU** to request, to ask		
	AFFIRMATIVE	NEGATIVE
	(tah-noh-mee-mahs)	(tah-noh-mee-mah-sehn)
PRESENT	tanomimasu	tanomimasen
	(tah-nohn-deh)	
PRESENT CONTINUOUS	tanonde imasu	tanonde imasen
	(tah-noh-mee-mahsh-tah)	
PAST	tanomimashita	tanomimasen deshita

Tokai de

(toh-kah-ee)

In the city

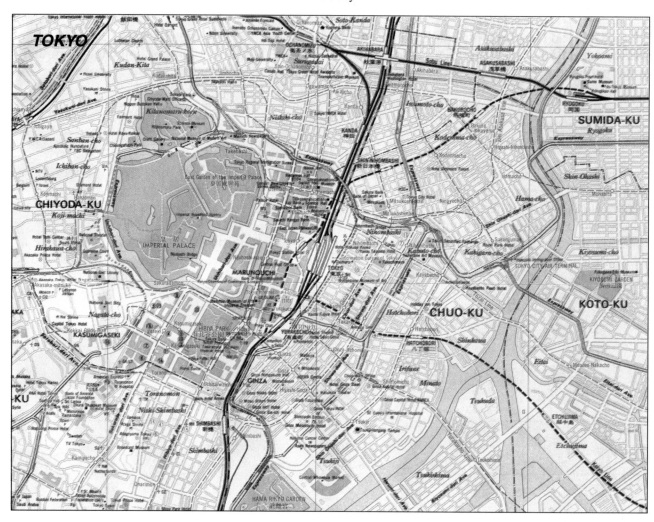

Back in Tokyo, Mark decides to do some sightseeing.

MARK **Sumimasen ga, Meiji** *(meh-jee)* **Jingū** *(jeen-goo)*

ga doko ni aru ka, oshiete

kudasai.

Excuse me, sir, can you tell me where the

Meiji Shrine is?

PASSERBY **Hai. Watakushi mo**

sotchi e ikimasu. Otsure *(soht-chee)* *(oh-tsoo-reh)*

shimashō. *(shee-mah-shoh)*

Yes. I'm going in that direction.

I'll show you.

106

MARK	**Arigatō gozaimasu.**	You're very kind.

MARK **Arigatō gozaimasu.** — You're very kind.

PASSERBY **Hoka no basho wa mimashita ka.** — Have you visited other sights yet?

(ah-sah-koo-sah)
MARK **Hai. Kinō wa, Asakusa** *(kahn-nohn)* **Kannon to Nakamise o mimashita. Sorekara** *(koh-KOO-ree-tsoo)* *(hah-koo-boo-tsoo-kahn)* **Kokuritsu Hakubutsukan e ikimashita.** — Yes. Yesterday we saw the Kannon Temple in Asakusa and the Nakamise arcade. Then we went to the Tokyo National Museum.

(ee-tah) *(nah-rah)*
PASSERBY **Ueno ni ita nara,** *(tah-boon)* *(dōh-boo-tsoo-ehn)* *(eet-tah)* **tabun dōbutsuen ni itta** *(deh-shoh)* **desho.** — And since you were in the Ueno area, you probably went to the zoo, right?

(pahn-dah)
MARK **Hai, ikimashita. Panda** *(mee-TAH-kaht-tah)* **o mitakatta kara desu.** — Yes, we did. We wanted to see the pandas.

(soh-toh)
PASSERBY **Tokyo no soto de, nanika mimashita ka.** — Have you seen any of the countryside outside Tokyo?

(kah-mah-koo-rah)
MARK **Kamakura de, Daibutsu o mimashita. Soshite ashita** *(eep-pah-koo)* **Hakone ni itte, ippaku shimasu.** — We've been to see the Daibutsu in Kamakura. And we're going to Hakone tomorrow for an overnight stay.

(keet-toh)(tah-noh-shēē)
PASSERBY **Kitto, tanoshii desu** *(yah-mah)* *(mee-zoo-oo-mee)* **yo. Yama to mizuumi ga** *(foo-jee-sahn)* **kirei desu. Tabun Fujisan ga yoku miemasu yo.** — You'll enjoy it. The mountains and lakes are beautiful. And you'll probably get a good view of Mount Fuji.

(soo-bah-rah-shee-sōh)
MARK **Subarashisō desu ne.** — It sounds wonderful.

PASSERBY   *(ah)*
A, koko ga Meiji   Well, here's the Meiji Shrine. Just go through the
(toh-ree-ee) (koo-goot-teh)
Jingū desu. Torii o kugutte   big tori gate. Have a good time!

ikimasu. Otanoshimi kudasai.

MARK   **Tasukete itadaite,**   Thanks for your help. I really appreciate it.

arigatō gozaimasu. Hontō ni,
(kahn-shah)
kansha shimasu.

Can you answer these True-False questions based on the dialogue?

1. Māku san wa, Meiji Jingū ni ikitai desu. _____ .

2. Kokuritsu Hakubutsukan e ikimasen deshita. _____ .

3. Meiji Jingū wa, Kamakura ni arimasu. _____ .

4. Daibutsu wa, Kamakura ni arimasu. _____ .

5. Hakone no yama to mizuumi ga kirei desu. _____ .

ENTERTAINMENT

12	(ehn-geh-kee) **Engeki** Theater	(eh-gah) **Eiga** Movies	(shoo-koo-jee-tsoo) **Shukujitsu** Holidays

ENGEKI
The Theater

The Smiths want to see a performance of the traditional Japanese theater while they're in Tokyo—they just can't decide which one!

MARK   **Konban, nani o shitai** *(shtah-ee)*

       desu ka.

What do you feel like doing tonight?

MARY   **Kabuki** *(kah-boo-kee)* **gekijō** *(geh-kee-joh)* **wa dō desu**

       ka.

How about going to the Kabuki Theater?

MARK   **Kabuki. Sore wa gōka na** *(goh-kah)*

       ishō *(ee-shoh)* **to dentō** *(dehn-toh)* **teki na** *(teh-kee)* **Nihon**

       no ongaku *(ohn-gah-koo)* **ga aru engeki desu**

       ka.

Kabuki? Is that with the fancy costumes and traditional Japanese music?

MARY   **Hai. Soretomo Bunraku o** *(boon-rah-koo)*

       mi ni iku koto mo dekimasu.

       Sore wa, ayatsuri *(ah-yah-tsoo-ree)* **ningyō** *(neen-gyoh)* **ga**

       aru engeki desu.

Yes. Or we could go to see a Bunraku play.

That's the one with the puppets.

MARK **Watakushi wa, ayatsuri**

ningyō ga kirai desu. Noh

wa, dō desu ka.

I don't like puppets. What about Noh?

(oh-mehn) *(tskah-oo)*
MARY **Omen o tsukau engeki desu**
(kehk-koh)
ka. Kekkō desu. Watakushi wa
(shee-mahs)
Kabuki ni shimasu.

The one with the masks? No thank you. I'll take Kabuki.

(kahn-gah-eh-teh)(mee-roo) *(doh-noh)*
MARK **Kangaete   miru to, dono**

engeki mo yaku go jikan
(kah-kah-ree-mahs)
kakarimasu. Konban no ken o
(tah-meh)
kau tame niwa, tabun
(oh-soh-soo-gee-roo) (deh-shoh)
ososugiru   deshō.

Now that I think of it, these performances are about five hours long. And it's probably too late to get tickets for tonight.

(bahn-goh-hahn)
MARY **Soredewa oishii bangohan**

o tabete, sorekara eiga ni

ikimashō.

Let's have a nice dinner and then go to a movie!

Now match the Japanese expressions with their English equivalents.

1. ayatsuri ningyō
2. engeki
3. kirai desu
4. ongaku
5. oishii bangohan

a. don't like
b. músic
c. a nice dinner
d. performance, theater
e. puppets

Bunpō o shōshō

Some grammar

DIRECT AND INDIRECT OBJECTS

In Units 2 and 4 you learned about **particles**. And you've been using them ever since. Let's review the **object particles**, or **object markers**, as they're also called. Remember? They're easy.

> **o** (and sometimes **ga**) for **direct object** and **ni** for **indirect object**.

Let's look at a few examples:

Watakushi **ni** sore **o** kudasai.
↓ ↓ ↓ ↓
me to it please give
Please give it to me.

Suchuwādesu wa, Māku san **ni** ocha **o** agemashita.
↓ ↓ ↓ ↓ ↓
stewardess Mark to tea gave
The stewardess gave Mark some tea.

Merī san wa suchuwādesu **ni** makura **o** tanomimashita.
↓ ↓ ↓ ↓ ↓
Mary stewardess to pillow asked
Mary asked the stewardess for a pillow.

Keikan wa Māku san **ni** michi **o** oshiemashita.
↓ ↓ ↓ ↓ ↓
policeman Mark to road explained
The policeman explained the road to Mark.

Can you supply the direct and indirect object particles?

1. Māku san wa Tanaka san _____ kore _____ agemashita.

2. Watakushi _____ ocha _____ kudasai.

3. Mēri san wa keikan _____ michi _____ kikimasu.
                                                  asks

ANSWERS

Particles 1. ni, o 2. ni, o 3. ni, o

111

EIGA
The Movies

(At the hotel, Mark and Mary are discussing what movie they plan to see.)

MARY **Donna eiga o mitai desu ka.**

Which movie do you want to see?

MARK **Moshi Nihon no eiga o mitara, wakarimasen.**

If we see a Japanese film, we won't understand it.

MARY **Soredewa, onsei ga** *(ohn-seh)* **orijinaru no Amerika eiga o** *(oh-ree-jee-nah-roo)* **mita hō ga ii deshō.**

Then we'd better see an American movie with an original soundtrack.

MARK **Hoteru no chikaku de, Amerika eiga o yatte imasu.** *(yaht-teh)*

I think there's an American film near the hotel.

MARY **Sore wa subarashii. Ikimashō.**

Good. Let's go.

(At the movie theater.)

MARY **Mae no hō ni, suwarimashō.** *(soo-wah-ree-mah-shoh)*

Let's sit toward the front.

MARK **Tama ni eigo o kiku no mo,** *(tah-mah)* **ii desu ne.**

It will be nice to hear English for a change.

MARY **Tashika ni. Kite yokatta** *(tahsh-kah)* *(yoh-kaht-tah)* **desu.**

It certainly will. I'm glad we came.

112

MARK	**Keredomo, ken wa**	The tickets were outrageously expensive, though.
	(moh-noh-soo-goh-koo)	
	monosugoku takai deshita.	

	(dah-reh-moh) (ee-oo)	
MARY	**A, sore wa daremo ga iu**	Well, as everyone says, this is Japan!
	(yoh)	
	yō ni, koko ga Nihon dakara	
	desu yo.	

Can you supply the missing Japanese from the dialogue?

1. Donna _____ o mitai desu ka.

2. _____ Nihon no eiga o mitara, wakarimasen.

3. _____ , onsei ga orijinaru no Amerika eiga o mita hō ga ii deshō.

4. Hoteru no _____ de, Amerika eiga o yatte imasu.

5. Sore wa subarashii. _____ .

(shoo-koo-jee-tsoo)
SHUKUJITSU
Holidays

While he's in Japan, Mark wants to know about the Japanese holidays.

Let's see what Mark's friend Mr. Tanaka has to say about them.

MARK	**Nihonjin wa, Amerikajin**	Do the Japanese celebrate the same holidays as
	(ee-wah-oo) (oh-nah-jee)	
	ga iwau shukujitsu to onaji	Americans do?
	(ee-wah-ee-mahs)	
	shukujitsu o iwaimasu ka.	

ANSWERS

Dialogue 1. eiga 2. Moshi 3. Soredewa 4. chikaku 5. Ikimashō

MR. TANAKA   Kurisumasu wa, Nihon *(koo-ree-soo-mahs)*

no shukujitsu dewa arimasen.

Keredomo, Nihonjin

wa oiwai ga   daisuki   dashi, *(oh-ee-wah-ee)(dah-ee-skee)(dah-shee)*

okurimono o   agetari, *(oh-koo-ree-moh-noh)(ah-geh-tah-ree)*

morattari suru no ga suki desu. *(moh-raht-tah-ree)*

Sorede, Kurisumasu o iwau *(soh-reh-deh)*

hito ga ōzei imasu. *(oh-zeh)*

Well, Christmas isn't a Japanese holiday. But Japanese love to celebrate, and we love to give and receive gifts. So many of us do enjoy Christmas.

MARK   Shinnen wa dō desu ka. *(sheen-nehn)*

What about the New Year?

MR. TANAKA   Shinnen wa, ichinen

de ichiban ōkii shukujitsu *(ee-chee-bahn)*

desu. Sore wa ōmisoka no ban *(oh-mee-soh-kah)*

ni hajimari, ichigatsu no *(hah-jee-mah-ree)*

saisho no mikka kan *(sah-ee-shoh)*

tsuzukimasu. Gakkō, kaisha, *(tsoo-zoo-kee-mahs)(kah-ee-shah)*

yakusho, soshite daibubun no *(yahk-shoh)(dah-ee-boo-boon)*

mise ga shimarimasu. *(shee-mah-ree-mahs)*

That's our biggest holiday of the year. It begins on New Year's Eve, and it continues for the first three days of January. Schools, businesses, government offices, and most stores are closed.

MARK   Shinnen wa, dō yatte

iwaimasu ka.

How do you celebrate?

MR. TANAKA   Kuru toshi no kenkō *(toh-shee)(kehn-kō)*

to kōun o inoru tame ni, *(kō-oon)(ee-noh-roo)*

takusan no hitotachi ga otera *(tahk-sahn)(hee-toh-tah-chee)(oh-teh-rah)*

ya jinja o otozuremasu. Kono *(jeen-jah)(oh-toh-zoo-reh-mahs)*

hi no tame ni, kimono o kiru *(kee-moh-noh)(kee-roo)*

Many people visit Buddhist temples and Shinto shrines to pray for good health and good luck for the coming year. Some wear kimono for the occasion. After that we visit homes of friends and relatives. We eat New Year's food, including

hito mo imasu. Omairi no
(oh-mah-ee-ree)

(ah-toh) (toh-moh-dah-chee) (sheen-seh-kee)
ato, tomodachi ya shinseki

o hōmon shimasu. Soshite
(hoh-mohn)

(moosh-tah)   (tsoo-ee-teh)
mushita okome o tsuite

(tskoot-tah)   (oh-moh-chee) (foo-koo-meh-teh)
tsukutta   omochi o fukumete,

shinnen no tabemono o

(tah-beh-mahs)
tabemasu.

MARK   **Hoka niwa, donna**

shukujitsu ga arimasu ka.

MR. TANAKA   **Takusan**

arimasu yo. Shi gatsu nijū

(mee-doh-ree)
ku nichi wa midori no hi, go

(kehn-poh)
gatsu mikka wa kenpō kinenbi,

go gatsu itsuka wa kodomo no

hi desu. Kono kikan wa,

(goh-roo-dehn) (wee-koo) (toh-shteh)   (shee-rah-reh-teh)
gōruden   wīku   toshite   shiraete

imasu.

(oh-MOH-shee-roh-ee)
MARK   **Omoshiroi desu ne.**

MR. TANAKA   **Chotto matte**

kudasai. Motto arimasu yo.

(keh-roh)
Ku gastu jūgo nichi wa keirō

(toh-SHEE-yoh-ree)
no hi desu. Toshiyori no

(sheen-seh-kee)
shinseki ya tomodachi o hōmon

(yoo-shoh-koo) (tsoo-reh-teh)
shite, yūshoku ni tsurete

ikikasu.

omochi, a special rice cake made of pounded,

steamed rice.

What other holidays do you have?

There are many. April 29th is Greenery Day, May

3rd is Constitution Day, and May 5th is

Children's Day. That period is known as Golden

Week.

How interesting!

Wait. There's more. September 15th is Respect

for the Aged Day. People visit elderly relatives

and friends and take them to dinner.

MARK *(deh-moh)*
MARK **Amerika demo, sore ga**
(ah-reh-bah)
areba ii to omoimasu.

I wish we had that one in the States!

(keen-rōh)
MR. TANAKA **Kinrō kansha no hi**

ga jūichi gatsu nijū san
(tehn-nōh) *(tahn-jōh-bee)*
nichi, tennō tanjōbi ga jūni

gatsu nijū san nichi desu.

Labor Thanksgiving Day is November 23rd, and

the Emperor's Birthday is December 23rd.

Can you match the dates with the Japanese holidays?

1. September 15
2. December 23
3. April 29
4. January 1
5. May 5
6. November 23

a. kinrō kansha no hi
b. kodomo no hi
c. midori no hi
d. shinnen
e. tennō tanjōbi
f. keirō no hi

116

(hah-ee-keen-goo)   *(joh-geen-goo)*
HAIKINGU TO JOGINGU
Hiking and Jogging

(Mark Smith is in great physical condition. He jogs every morning. Sometimes Mary, Anne, and Paul join him, but they can barely keep up. This morning he is approached by a reporter who is writing an article on sports.)

REPORTER   **Ohayō gozaimasu.**   Good morning, sir. I am a reporter. May I ask
(reh-poh-tah)
Watakushi wa, repōtā desu   you some questions?

ga. Shitsumon o shitemo ii

desu ka.

MARK   **Dōzo. Keredomo yukkuri**   Certainly. But speak slowly. I'm an American,

hanashite kudasai. Watakushi   and I don't understand everything.

wa Amerikajin de, zenbu wa

wakarimasen.

REPORTER   **Yoku jogingu o**   Do you jog often?

shimasu ka.

117

MARK   *(mah-ee)*
Hai. Mai asa shimasu.
(toh-kee-doh-kee)   *(ees-shoh)*
Tokidoki, kazoku mo issho ni

kimasu. Ushiro ni iru,
(toh-rēh-neen-goo) *(weh-ah)* *(kee-teh)*
torēningu   **wea o kite**
(rahn-neen-goo)   *(shōō-zoo)*
ranningu   **shūzu o**
(hah-ee-teh) *(ee-roo)*
haite   **iru no ga**

watakushi no kazoku desu.

REPORTER   **Hoka no supōtsu mo**

suki desu ka.

MARK   *(yah-kyōō)*
Yakyū to, tenisu to,
(sahk-kāh)
sakka o suru no ga suki desu.

REPORTER   **Haikingu wa dō**

desu ka.

MARK   **Haikingu wa daisuki desu.**

Watakushitachi wa, haikingu
(kyahn-peen-goo)
to kyanpingu o issho ni

shimasu. Watakushitachi wa,

surīpingu baggu to,
(ryook-koo-sahk-koo)   *(soo-ee-tōh)*
ryukkusakku to, suitō to,

ryōri yōgu o motte kimashita.

REPORTER   **Nihon e desu ka.**

MARK   **Hai. Watakushitachi wa**
(yah-mah-noh-boh-ree)
yamanobori mo suki desu.
(mōh-jee-kee)
Tabun, mōjiki Fujisan ni
(noh-boh-ree-mahs)
noborimasu.

Yes. Every morning. Sometimes my family comes

with me. There they are behind us, wearing

sweatshirts and running shoes.

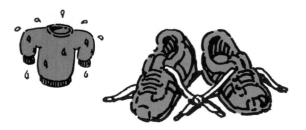

Do you like any other sports?

I like to play baseball, tennis, and soccer.

What about hiking?

I love hiking. We combine it with camping. We

brought our sleeping bags, backpacks, canteens,

and cooking utensils with us.

To Japan?

Yes. We even like mountain climbing. Maybe

we'll climb Mount Fuji soon.

REPORTER **Zuibun nozomi ga** *(zoo-ee-boon) (noh-zoh-mee)*
takai desu ne. Arigato
gozaimashita. Kōun o oinori *(Koh-oon) (oh-ee-noh-ree)*
shimasu.

You're very ambitious. Thank you and good luck.

After reading the dialogue several times, indicate if each of the following is true or false.

1. Māku san wa Amerikajin de, zenbu wakarimasu. 1. _____

2. Mai asa joggingu shimasu. 2. _____

3. Tokidoki, kazoku mo issho ni kimasu. 3. _____

4. Māku san wa yakyū to, tenisu to, sakkā o suru no ga kirai desu. 4. _____

5. Haikingu wa daisuki desu. 5. _____

6. Karera wa, haikingu to kyanpingu o issho ni shimasen. 6. _____

7. Surīpingu baggu to, ryukkusakku to, suitō to, ryōri yōgu o motte kimasen deshita. 7. _____

8. Māku san wa yamanobori mo suki desu. 8. _____

9. Fujisan ni noboritai desu. 9. _____

10. Māku san no nozomi ga takakunai desu. 10. _____

119

Bunpō chūshaku
(chōo-shah-koo)
Grammar note

Notice how everyday expressions using adjectives may take very different forms in English and in Japanese!

English: I'm hungry.
Japanese: My stomach is empty.

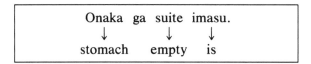

English: You're very ambitious.
Japanese: Your ambition is very high, isn't it?

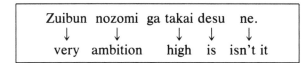

English: I'm thirsty.
Japanese: My throat is dry.

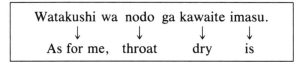

Note that **Watakushi wa** is translated as "As for me." This may be helpful for you to keep in mind as you proceed with your study of Japanese.

Are you ready for a hiking trip now? Let's see if you can identify this gear.

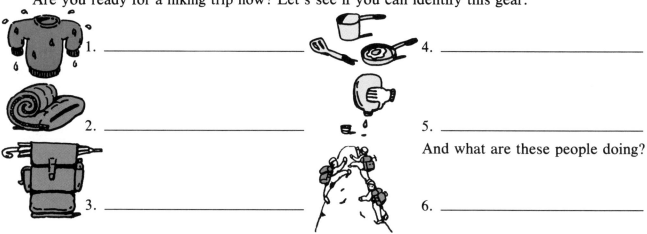

1. _____
2. _____
3. _____
4. _____
5. _____

And what are these people doing?

6. _____

SAIKURINGU TO SUIE

(sah-ee-koo-reen-goo) (soo-ee-eh)

Bicycling and Swimming

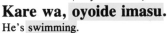

(noh-boh-ree-zah-kah) (jee-tehn-shah) (ohsh-teh)

Kanojo wa, noborizaka de jitensha o oshite imasu.

She's pushing the bicycle uphill.

(boh-foo) (meh-gah-neh) (kah-keh-teh)

Karera wa, bōfū megane o kakete imasu.

They're wearing goggles.

(oh-yoh-ee-deh)

Kare wa, oyoide imasu.

He's swimming.

(hee-rah-oh-yoh-gee)

hiraoyogi

breaststroke

(koo-rōh-roo)

kurōru

crawl

(hah-ee-eh)

haiei

backstroke

And let's not forget nature!

(ksah)

kusa

plants

(hah-nah)

hana

flowers

(moo-shee)

mushi

insects

(dōh-boo-tsoo)

dōbutsu

animals

Supply the missing Japanese for each sentence.

1. Karera wa, _____ o kakete imasu.
   <u>goggles</u>

2. Kare wa, _____ .
   <u>is swimming</u>

Now answer the questions.

1. Kore wa nan desu ka.   K_____.

2. Kore wa nan desu ka.   K_____.

3. Kore wa hana desu ka.   Iie,_____.

4. Kore wa mushi desu ka.   Iie,_____.

ORDERING FOOD
(tah-beh-moh-noh)   *(choo-mohn)*
Tabemono no Chūmon

| 14 | *(shoh-koo-jee)*
 Shokuji/Tabemono
 Meals   Food | |

You're going to be eating a lot of different food in Japan, so it's time to learn the expressions you'll need.

First of all, two *essential* verbs.

(doh-shee)   *(oh)*   *(moh)*   *(skoh-shee)*
Dōshi o mō sukoshi
      More Verbs

	(tah-beh-roo) **TABERU** to eat	
	AFFIRMATIVE	**NEGATIVE**
PRESENT	tabemasu	*(tah-beh-mah-sehn)* tabemasen
PRESENT CONTINUOUS	*(tah-beh-teh)* tabete imasu	tabete imasen
PAST	*(tah-beh-mahsh-tah)* tabemashita	tabemasen deshita

	(noh-moo) **NOMU** to drink	
	AFFIRMATIVE	**NEGATIVE**
PRESENT	*(noh-mee-mahs)* nomimasu	*(noh-mee-mah-sehn)* nomimasen
PRESENT CONTINUOUS	*(nohn-deh)* nonde imasu	nonde imasen
PAST	*(noh-mee-mahsh-tah)* nomimashita	nomimasen deshita

Now you're ready for some eating adventures!

You can get almost any kind of food you want in Japan. You'll want to try Japanese food, of course, but you'll welcome familiar western food as well. A western meal could be similar to food you would have in the United States—anything from a simple sandwich to a steak with all the trimmings. The western food in Japan is good and varied. You'll find American-style pizza, burgers, and fried chicken, French haute cuisine, Italian restaurants, and much more.

Let's start with breakfast. A Japanese breakfast includes a bowl of hot rice, a raw egg, some soybean soup, seaweed, perhaps some fish, pickles, and, of course, green tea.

A Japanese-style lunch is usually light. Most popular is a simple bowl of noodles (there are many varieties) with a bit of fish or meat and a few vegetables served in a savory broth.

A typical Japanese dinner consists of a variety of small dishes, including vegetables, meat, poultry, or seafood, rice, soup, pickles, and tea. Dessert, if any, is usually fruit.

You'll find a listing of Japanese foods in the food guide at the back of this book.

(ah-sah   goh-hahn)
ASA GOHAN
Breakfast

(The Smiths are having a western-style breakfast at a local, inexpensive restaurant.)

(tah-kah-koo-nah-ee)
takakunai
inexpensive

(reh-soo-toh-rahn)
resutoran
restaurant

MARK **Asa gohan o takusan**
(tah-beh-tah-ee)
tabetai desu.

I'm ready for a big breakfast.

MARY **Watakushi mo, onaka ga**

suite imasu.

I'm hungry too.

WAITRESS **Ohayō gozaimasu.**
(goh-chōo-mohn) (oo-KAH-gah-ee-mah-shōh)
Gochūmon o ukagaimashō ka.

Good morning. May I take your order?

(hah-jee-meh)
MARK **Hajime ni, kōhī o onegai**

shimasu.

Could you bring coffee first, please?

WAITRESS **Hai, dōzo. Kore ga**
(mee-roo-koo) (oh-sah-tōh)
miruku to osatō desu.

Here you are. And here are the cream and sugar.

123

MARK **Arigatō. Kōhī ga totemo**
(noh-mee-tah-kaht-tah) (koh-reh-deh)
nomitakatta desu. Korede,
(chōo-mohn)
chūmon dekimasu.

Thanks. I needed that. Now we can order.

(toh-stoh)
MARY **Watakushi niwa, tōsuto**
(oh-rehn-jee)
to orenji jūsu o kudasai.

I'll have toast and a glass of orange juice.

(oh-toh-mēe-roo)
MARK **Watakushi niwa, ōtomīru**
(meh-DAH-mah-yah-kee)
to, medamayaki o futatsu,
(bēh-kohn) (toh-mah-toh)
bēkon, tōsuto, soshite tomato

jūsu o kudasai.

I'll have oatmeal, two fried eggs with bacon,

toast, and some tomato juice, please.

(shee-ree-ah-roo)
ANNE **Watakushi niwa, shiriaru**
(roh-roo) (goo-rēh-poo-foo-rōo-tsoo)
to, rōru pan to, gurēpufurūtsu

o kudasai.

I'd like cereal, breakfast rolls, and grapefruit.

PAUL **Watakushi niwa, orenji**
(hoht-toh) (kēh-kee) (soh-seh-jee)
jūsu to, hotto kēki to sōsēji
(mee-roo-koo)
to miruku o kudasai.

I'll have orange juice and pancakes with sausage,

and some milk, please.

(meen-nah) (mee-zoo)
MARK **Minna ni mizu o**
onegai shimasu.

We'd all like some water, please.

(bah-tāh) (jah-moo)
MARY **Batā to jamu o kudasai.**

Could you bring us some butter and jam?

(The Smiths finish their breakfast.)

(oh-kahn-jōh)
MARK **Sumimasen ga, okanjō o**
onegai shimasu.

Waitress, the check, please.

WAITRESS **Hai, dōzo. Arigatō**

gozaimashita.

Here you are, sir. Thank you.

Can you fill in the blanks with the correct Japanese expressions?

1. _____ o kudasai.   (orange juice and toast)

2. Watakushi niwa, kōhī o _____ .   (please)

3. _____ , jūsu o onegai shimasu.   (first)

4. Batā o _____ kudasai.   (some more)

5. _____ o onegai shimasu.   (the check)

Ordering in Japanese is easy! Here are a few more tips:

If you're alone, you don't need the pronoun, **watakushi**. You can say either

> **Medamayaki o futatsu to bēkon o kudasai.**

or

> **Tōsuto to kōhī o onegai shimasu.**

You can use either **kudasai** or **onegai shimasu** when ordering. If you're in a group, use **watakushi niwa** when giving your order.

> **Watakushi niwa, tomato jūsu o kudasai.**

> **Watakushi niwa, hotto kēki to sōsēji o onegai shimasu.**

Since you'll be having both western and Japanese-style meals, you should learn the following words that describe them:

> *(yōh-shoh-koo)*
> **yōshoku**   western food

> *(wah-shoh-koo)*
> **washoku**   Japanese food

TĒBURU
The Table

When the Smiths dine out, their place settings may look like this one. When you have read and pronounced the vocabulary, try to identify each object in the picture without referring to the Japanese word.

(kohp-poo)
koppu
glass

(wah-een)   *(goo-rah-soo)*
wain   gurasu
wine glass

(jah-wahn)
kōhī jawan
coffee cup

(shee-oh) *(koh-shoh)*
shio to koshō
salt and pepper

(oh-sah-toh)
osatō
sugar

(oo-keh-zah-rah)
ukezara
saucer

(nah-poo-keen)
napukin
napkin

(foh-koo)
fōku
fork

(soo-poon)
supūn
spoon

(oh-sah-rah)
osara
plate

(nah-ee-foo)
naifu
knife

(yah-koo-dah-tsoo)   *(hyoh-gehn)*
Yakudatsu hyōgen
Some helpful expressions

You'll be able to use these expressions often when dining.

(skoh-shee) **sukoshi**	some, a little
(moh skoh-shee) **mō sukoshi**	a little more
(moht-toh) **motto**	more
(tahk-sahn) **takusan**	a lot

Without looking at the picture, match up the two columns.

1. wain gurasu		a. plate
2. napukin		b. glass
3. koshō		c. saucer
4. osara		d. coffee cup
5. fōku		e. knife
6. supūn		f. fork
7. osatō		g. wine glass
8. kōhī jawan		h. napkin
9. ukezara		i. pepper
10. koppu		j. sugar
11. naifu		k. salt
12. shio		l. spoon

(goh-ee)
Goi o mō sukoshi
More vocabulary

(noh-mee-moh-noh)
nomimono   beverage   **pan**   bread

(soh-foo-toh)(doh-reen-koo)
sofuto   dorinku   soft drink   **rōru pan**   rolls

(mee-neh-rah-roo) (woh-tah)
mineraru   wōtā   mineral water   **sūpu**   soup

(oh-doh-boo-roo)
mizu o ippai   a glass of water   **ōdoboru**   appetizers

(ah-SOO-pah-rah-gah-soo)
asuparagasu   asparagus   *(koo-dah-moh-noh)*
kudamono   fruit

(mahs-shoo-roo-moo)
masshurūmu   mushrooms   **ringo**   apples

ANSWERS

Matching 1. g 2. h 3. i 4. a 5. f 6. l 7. j 8. d 9. c 10. b 11. e. 12. k

127

(soh-seh-jee)
sōsēji — sausage

(nee-koo)
niku — meat

hamu — ham

(sah-kah-nah)
sakana — fish

(chee-keen)
chikin — chicken

(roh-stoh) *(bee-foo)*
rōsuto bīfu — roast beef

(yah-sah-ee)
yasai — vegetables

(neen-jeen)
ninjin — carrots

(kah-REE-foo-rah-wah)
karifurawā — cauliflower

(kyoo-ree)
kyūri — cucumber

(hoh-rehn-soh)
hōrensō — spinach

(sah-yah-een-gehn)
sayaingen — string beans

(oh-nee-ohn)
onion — onions

(mah-meh)
mame — peas

(rah-ee-soo)
raisu — rice (on a *plate*)

(toh-mah-toh)
tomato — tomatoes

(bah-nah-nah)
banana — bananas

(sah-KOO-rahn-boh)
sakuranbo — cherries

(ee-chee-goh)
ichigo — strawberries

(meh-rohn)
meron — melon

(soo-ee-kah)
suika — watermelon

(oh-rehn-jee)
orenji — oranges

(mee-kahn)
mikan — mandarin oranges

(goo-reh-poo-foo-roo-tsoo)
gurēpufurūtsu — grapefruit

(moh-moh)
momo — peaches

(nah-shee)
nashi — pears

(boo-doh)
budō — grapes

(boo-rahn-deh)
burandē — brandy

(eh-soo-poo-rehs-soh)
esupuresso — espresso

kōhī — coffee

(koh-chah)
kōcha — tea (western)

miruku — milk

128

(reh-tah-soo)		*(deh-zah-toh)*	
retasu	lettuce	**dezāto**	dessert

(sah-rah-dah)		*(meh-een) (koh-soo)*	
sarada	salad	**mein kōsu**	entree

Now that you know foods, remember the difference between **yōshoku** (western food) and **washoku** (Japanese food). This affects some of the names. For example, in western meals, rice (on a plate) is **raisu**. In Japanese meals, rice (in a rice bowl) is **gohan**. Western tea is **kōcha**, Japanese tea is **ocha**.

(nee-hohn)   *(teh-boo-roo)*

NIHON NO TĒBURU
The Japanese Table

(shoh-yoo) **shōyu** soy sauce

(yoh-jee) **yōji** toothpicks

(tohk-koo-ree) **tokkuri** sake jug

(sah-KAH-zoo-kee) **sakazuki** sake cup

(oh-chah-wahn) **ochawan** rice bowl

(oh-koh-zah-rah) **okozara** pickle dish

(yoo-noh-mee) (jah-wahn) **yunomi   jawan** teacup

okozara soy sauce dish

(oh-sah-rah) **osara** plate

(hah-shee) (oh-kee) **hashi   oki** chopstick rest

(oh-bohn) **obon** tray

(hah-shee) **hashi** chopsticks

(oh-wahn) **owan** soup bowl

You may already have tried some Japanese food at restaurants in the United States. If so, you know the names of some popular dishes to order—**sukiyaki,   sushi,   sashimi,   tempura,** *(skee-yah-kee) (soo-shee) (sah-shee-mee) (tehn-poo-rah)*

(yah-KEE-toh-ree) **yakitori.** For descriptions of these and other Japanese dishes and types of cuisine, see the food guide at the back of this book.

(The Smiths have decided to eat at an expensive restaurant.)

WAITER *(meh-nyōō)* **Konbanwa. Menyū o** *(goh-rahn)* **goran ni narimasu ka.**

Good evening.

Would you like to see the menu?

MARK **Hai, onegai shimasu.**

Yes, please.

WAITER **Konban wa oishii ōdoburu ga gozaimasu.** *(kohn-bee-neh-shohn)* *(oh-moh-chee)* **Konbinēshon o omochi shimashō ka.**

We have some delicious appetizers tonight. Shall I bring you an assortment?

MARK *(oh-ee-shee-sōh)* **Sore wa oishisō desu ne.**

That sounds wonderful.

MARY **Watakushi wa, ōdoburu wa kekkō desu. Saisho ni, sūpu o kudasai.**

No appetizers for me. For my first course, I'll have the soup.

WAITER *(meh-een)* *(kōh-soo)* **Mein kōsu wa, nani ni** *(nah-sah-ee-mahs)* **nasaimasu ka.**

And what would you like for your main course?

MARY *(poh-teh-toh)* **Chikin to poteto.** *(goo-rēēn)* **Sorekara gurīn sarada o onegai shimasu.**

I'll have chicken with potatoes. And a green salad.

MARK *(koh-oo-shee)* **Watakushi niwa, koushi** *(kah-TSOO-reh-tsoo)* *(meek-koo-soo)* **no katsuretsu to mikkusu sarada o kudasai.**

I'll have a veal cutlet and the mixed salad.

ANNE **Watakushi wa, daietto** *(dah-ee-eht-toh)* **chū** *(choo)*
desu. Sorede, *(soh-reh-deh)* **pan to chīzu** *(chee-zoo)*
dake kudasai. *(dah-keh)*

I'm on a diet. I'll just have some bread and cheese.

PAUL **Watakushi wa, yaki** *(yah-kee)* **zakana** *(zah-kah-nah)*
to, poteto to, ninjin o
onegai shimasu.

I'd like the broiled fish with potatoes and carrots.

(Toward the end of the meal)

WAITER **Hoka ni, nanika**
goiriyō desu ka. *(goh-ee-ree-yoh)*

Will there be anything else, sir?

MARK **Watakushi ni, mō sukoshi kōhī o**
kudasai. Sorekara, dezāto no menyū o
onegai shimasu.

I'd like some more coffee. And may we see the dessert menu, please?

(After the waiter brings the check)

MARY **Chippu o wasurenaide** *(wah-soo-ree-nah-ee-deh)*
kudasai.

Don't forget to leave a tip!

ANNE **Nihon dewa, chippu o**
ageru *(ah-geh-roo)* **hitsuyō wa nai to** *(hee-tsoo-yoh)* *(nah-ee)*
omoimashita.

I thought you don't have to tip in Japan.

MARK **Sābisu** *(sah-bee-soo)* **ryō wa, sudeni** *(ryoh)* *(see-deh-nee)*
haitte imasu.

The service charge is already included.

When you have read the dialogue aloud until you are familiar with it, try to complete the missing parts from these lines without looking back. Then check your answers.

1. _____ . Menyū o goran ni narimasu ka.

2. Watakushi wa, _____ kekkō desu. Saisho ni, _____ .

3. Watakushi wa, daietto chū desu. Sorede, _____ .

4. Watakushi ni, _____ kōhī o kudasai. Sorekara, _____

_____ .

(oh-teh-ah-rah-ee)
Otearai
Restrooms

After dinner, the Smiths want to freshen up.

otearai   restroom

(foo-jeen-yōh)
fujin yō
ladies

(sheen-shee yōh)
shinshi yō
gentlemen

Otearai wa doko desu ka.   Where's the restroom?

Here are some more items you might want to order in a restaurant in Japan.

Ōdoburu (Appetizers)	**Sūpu (Soups)**

(oh-moo-reh-tsoo)
omuretsu
omelet

(bee-shee-soh-ah)
bishisoa
vichyssoise

(mēe-toh-bōh-roo)
mītobōru
meatballs

onion sūpu
onion soup

Sarada (Salads)

mikkusu sarada
mixed salad

(rohs-shahn sah-rah-dah)
rosshan sarada
Russian salad

Sakana (Fish)

(ee-kah)
ika
squid

(eh-bee)
ebi
shrimp

Yasai (Vegetables)

asuparagasu
asparagus

hōrensō
spinach

Niku (Meat)

(poh-koo)
rōsuto pōku
roast pork

(koh-HEE-tsoo-jee)
kohitsuji
lamb

Nomimono (Drinks)

(oh-sah-keh)
osake
alcoholic beverages

(rehd-doh) (hoh-wah-ee-toh)
reddo/howaito wain
red/white wine

Dezāto (Desserts)

(ah-ee-skoo-rēē-moo)
aisukurīmu
ice cream

(pēh-stoh-rēē)
pēsutorī
pastries

To wrap up our section on eating out, fill in the menu with the Japanese words.

MENU

(fish)

(soup)

(chicken)

(salad)

(dessert)

(vegetable)

(wine)

ANSWERS

Menu sūpu (soup), sarada (salad), yasai (vegetables), sakana (fish), chikin (chicken), dezāto (dessert),

133

HOW'RE YOU DOING?

Dō desu ka.

We've covered a lot of ground so far, and now it's time for a breather! This section will help you to see where you are at this point. Have some fun with the activities, and if you've forgotten anything, just look it up. Are you ready?

First, let's try a verb review. Can you fill in the correct verb form in the following sentences?

1. Amerika kara _____ . (kuru)

2. Ashita, Tokyo ni _____ . (iku)

3. Sumisu san wa, kinō Kyoto ni _____ . (tsuku)

4. Ano hito wa, ima ban gohan o _____ . (taberu)

5. Watakushi wa, nihongo ga sukoshi _____ . (hanaseru)

6. Kono sukiyaki wa oishii _____ . (da)

7. Donna tenki _____ ka. (da)

8. Yukkuri _____ kudasai. (hanasu)

9. Yoku jogingu o _____ ka. (suru)

10. Nihongo ga suki _____ . (da)

Now let's check your knowledge of possessives. Fill in the indicated item in Japanese:

1. _____ pasupōto (my)

2. _____ kuruma (Mr. Tanaka's)

3. _____ hon (her)

4. _____ okusan (Mark's)

5. _____ ongaku (American)

Fill in the missing particles:

1. Māku san _____ , ban gohan _____ tabetai desu.

2. Merī san _____ , Amerika _____ kimashita.

3. Merī san _____ , ima Nihon _____ imasu.

4. Watakushi _____ kōhī _____ kudasai.

5. Tanaka san _____ , resutoran _____ asa gohan _____ tabete imasu.

Can you say these important expressions in Japanese?

1. I'm hungry. _____

2. I'm thirsty. _____

3. Where's the restroom? _____

Fill in the answers to the question below.

Ima nanji desu ka.

(1:15)

1. _____

(2:30)

2. _____

(3:45)

3. _____

(11:30)

4. _____

(7:20)

5. _____

(9:39)

6. _____

You're doing fine! See how it's all making sense? Now here's a crossword puzzle for you to enjoy:

ACROSS

1. child
3. tomorrow
4. speaks
6. comes
8. bullet train
9. one's self
12. that (adj.)
14. woman
15. breakfast
17. room
18. window

DOWN

2. Good morning
5. taxi
7. does
10. what
11. November
13. Japanese language
16. from

Look at the following flags and write the Japanese for the name of the country, the nationality, and the language.

1. ————————— , ————————— , —————————

2. ————————— , ————————— , —————————

3. ————————— , ————————— , —————————

Now match the items on the left with the ones on the right.

1. Konnichiwa.

2. Dōmo arigatō gozaimasu.

3. Kisha wa, nanji ni demasu ka.

4. Donna tenki desu ka.

5. Konban, nani o shitai desu ka.

6. Sumimasen ga, okanjō o kudasai.

7. Kankō kyaku desu ka.

8. Nihongo ga dekimasu ka.

a. Sukoshi dekimasu.

b. Eiga ni ikimashō.

c. Hai, dōzo.

d. Konnichiwa.

e. Atatakai desu.

f. Iie, dō itashimashite.

g. Hai, sō desu.

h. Kuji han ni demasu.

AT THE STORE
(mee-seh)
Mise de

| 16 | *(yōh-foo-koo   yah)* *(sah-ee-zoo)* *(kee-hohn   teh-kee   nah) (ee-roh)*
 Yōfuku ya / Saizu / Kihon teki na iro
 Clothing Stores/Sizes/Basic Colors |

(yōh-foo-koo)   *(tah-mehs)*
YŌFUKU O TAMESU
Trying on Clothes

You can't leave Japan without doing some shopping. How about a lovely Japanese kimono? And for western-style clothing, Japanese designers rival the world's best. Yes, they can be pricey, but you'll find something to suit your budget.

(ah-oh-ee)(zoo-bohn)   (hah-ee-teh)
Kare wa, aoi   zubon o haite imasu.
He's wearing blue pants.

(mee-doh-ree)   (wahn-pee-soo)   (kee-teh)
Kanojo wa, midori iro no wanpīsu o   kite imasu.
She's wearing a green dress.

For trying on clothes, you'll need to know some verbs. And you may be in for a bit of a surprise. In English, we say "put on" and "take off" for any item of clothing. In Japanese, we use different verbs for different items of clothing. The key factor, for the most part, is the part of the body where the item is worn. Here's a chart showing how it works, followed by the tenses for each new verb:

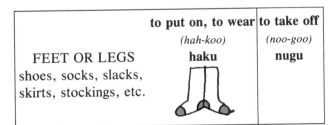

	to put on, to wear	to take off
	(hah-koo)	*(noo-goo)*
FEET OR LEGS shoes, socks, slacks, skirts, stockings, etc.	**haku**	**nugu**

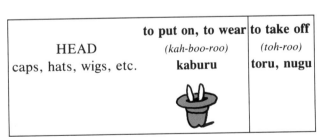

	to put on, to wear	to take off
HEAD caps, hats, wigs, etc.	*(kah-boo-roo)* **kaburu**	*(toh-roo)* **toru, nugu**

	to put on, to wear	to take off
	(kee-roo)	
TORSO sweaters, dresses, shirts, blouses, jackets, coats, etc.	**kiru**	**nugu**

	to put on, to wear	to take off
	(shee-meh-roo)	
BELTS AND NECKTIES	**shimeru**	**toru**

Fortunately, you can use **tamesu,** *(tah-mehs)* ''to try on'' for *any* item of clothing.

tamesu *to try on*		
	AFFIRMATIVE	NEGATIVE
PRESENT	*(tah-meh-shee-mahs)* **tameshimasu**	*(tah-meh-shee-mah-sehn)* **tameshimasen**
PRESENT CONTINUOUS	*(tah-mehsh-teh)* **tameshite imasu**	**tameshite imasen**
PAST	*(tah-meh-shee-mahsh-tah)* **tameshimashita**	**tameshimasen deshita**

haku *to put on, to wear*		
	AFFIRMATIVE	NEGATIVE
PRESENT	*(hah-kee-mahs)* **hakimasu**	*(hah-kee-mah-sehn)* **hakimasen**
PRESENT CONTINUOUS	*(hah-ee-teh)* **haite imasu**	**haite imasen**
PAST	*(hah-kee-mahsh-tah)* **hakimashita**	**hakimasen deshita**

kiru *to put on, to wear*		
	AFFIRMATIVE	NEGATIVE
PRESENT	*(kee-mahs)* **kimasu**	*(kee-mah-sehn)* **kimasen**
PRESENT CONTINUOUS	*(kee-teh)* **kite imasu**	**kite imasen**
PAST	*(kee-mahsh-tah)* **kimashita**	**kimasen deshita**

kaburu *to put on, to wear*		
	AFFIRMATIVE	NEGATIVE
PRESENT	*(kah-boo-ree-mahs)* **kaburimasu**	*(kah-boo-ree-mah-sehn)* **kaburimasen**
PRESENT CONTINUOUS	*(kah-boot-teh)* **kabutte imasu**	**kabutte imasen**
PAST	*(kah-boo-ree-mahsh-tah)* **kaburimashita**	**kaburimasen deshita**

shimeru		
to put on, to wear		
	AFFIRMATIVE	**NEGATIVE**
	(shee-meh-mahs)	*(shee-meh-mah-sehn)*
PRESENT	**shimemasu**	**shimemasen**
	(shee-meh-teh)	
PRESENT CONTINUOUS	**shimete imasu**	**shimete imasen**
	(shee-meh-mahsh-tah)	
PAST	**shimemashita**	**shimemasen deshita**

nugu		
to take off, to remove		
	AFFIRMATIVE	**NEGATIVE**
	(noo-gee-mahs)	*(noo-gee-mah-sehn)*
PRESENT	**nugimasu**	**nugimasen**
	(noo-ee-deh)	
PRESENT CONTINUOUS	**nuide imasu**	**nuide imasen**
	(noo-gee-mahsh-tah)	
PAST	**nugimashita**	**nugimasen deshita**

toru		
to take off, to remove		
	AFFIRMATIVE	**NEGATIVE**
	(toh-ree-mahs)	*(toh-ree-mah-sehn)*
PRESENT	**torimasu**	**torimasen**
	(toht-teh)	
PRESENT CONTINUOUS	**totte imasu**	**totte imasen**
	(toh-ree-mahsh-tah)	
PAST	**torimashita**	**torimasen deshita**

To shop for clothing, the verbs ''to need'' and ''to fit'' will be invaluable. For these expressions, of course, you don't use the present continuous form.

(ee-roo) **iru** to need		
	AFFIRMATIVE	**NEGATIVE**
	(ee-ree-mahs)	*(ee-ree-mah-sehn)*
PRESENT	**irimasu**	**irimasen**
	(ee-ree-mahsh-tah)	
PAST	**irimashita**	**irimasen deshita**

(ah-oo) **au** to fit		
	AFFIRMATIVE	**NEGATIVE**
	(ah-ee-mahs)	*(ah-ee-mah-sehn)*
PRESENT	**aimasu**	**aimasen**
	(ah-ee-mahsh-tah)	
PAST	**aimashita**	**aimasen deshita**

Let's try a few of the verbs you just learned. Look at the picture, and write the present continuous verb form.

	putting on	taking off
1.	1. _____	_____
2.	2. _____	_____
3.	3. _____	_____
4.	4. _____	_____

(sheen-shee   foo-koo)

SHINSHI FUKU
Men's Clothes

Here are the Japanese words for basic items of men's clothing.

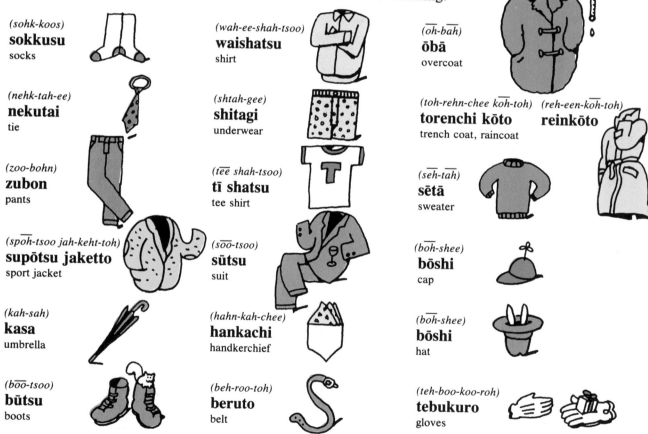

(sohk-koos)
sokkusu
socks

(nehk-tah-ee)
nekutai
tie

(zoo-bohn)
zubon
pants

(spoh-tsoo jah-keht-toh)
supōtsu jaketto
sport jacket

(kah-sah)
kasa
umbrella

(boo-tsoo)
būtsu
boots

(wah-ee-shah-tsoo)
waishatsu
shirt

(shtah-gee)
shitagi
underwear

(tee shah-tsoo)
tī shatsu
tee shirt

(soo-tsoo)
sūtsu
suit

(hahn-kah-chee)
hankachi
handkerchief

(beh-roo-toh)
beruto
belt

(oh-bah)
ōbā
overcoat

(toh-rehn-chee koh-toh)
torenchi kōto

(reh-een-koh-toh)
reinkōto
trench coat, raincoat

(seh-tah)
sētā
sweater

(boh-shee)
bōshi
cap

(boh-shee)
bōshi
hat

(teh-boo-koo-roh)
tebukuro
gloves

142

While in Tokyo, the Smiths are invited to a party, and Mark needs a suit. He goes to a men's clothing store in Ginza to buy one.

CLERK   **Nanika, goiriyō desu ka.**

May I help you?

MARK   **Sūtsu ga, irimasu. Sore**
(ah-oo)
ni au waishatsu mo

irimasu. Watakushi no

Amerika no saizu wa 42 desu.

I need a suit. And a dress shirt to go with it. My American size is 42.

(kohn)

CLERK   **Wakarimashita. Kono kon no**

sūtsu o tameshite kudasai.
(eh-roo)
Eru saizu desu. Kore wa,
(hah-zoo)
au kazu desu.

Fine. Try this dark blue one on. It's a Large. It should fit you.

(peet-tah-ree)

MARK   **Pittari desu. Kore o**
(ee-tah-dah-kee-mahs)
itadakimasu. Kore ni au

nekutai o ippon to, sokkusu o
(ees-soh-koo)
issoku to, hankachi o ichi

mai kudasai.

This fits perfectly. I'll take it. And a tie, socks, and a handkerchief to go with it.

CLERK   **Okanjō o dōzo. Yon jū**
(nee nah-ree-mahs)
go man en ni narimasu.

Here's your bill, sir. That will be 450,000 yen.

(meh-mah-ee)

MARK   **Chotto, memai ga shimasu.**
(yoo-kah) *(tah-oh-reh-teh)*
[Kare wa, yuka ni taorete

shimaimasu.]

I'm feeling a little dizzy . . . [He sinks to the floor.]

CLERK   **Tasukete kudasai.**
(kee oh
Okyaku sama ga ki o
oo-shee-naht-teh)
ushinatte shimaimashita.

Help! My customer has just fainted!

Can you answer these questions about the dialogue?

Māku san wa, nani ga irimasu ka.

1. _____

Kare no saizu wa, nan desu ka.

2. _____

Sūtsu wa, nani iro desu ka.

3. _____

Māku san wa, naze ki o ushinatte shimaimashita ka.

4. _____

Okanjo wa, ikura desu ka.

5. _____

(sah-ee-zoo)
Saizu
Sizes

(sheen-shee foo-koo) (noh) (sah-ee-zoo)
Shinshi fuku no saizu
Men's Clothing Sizes

WAISHATSU (SHIRTS)

American Size	14	14½	15	15½	16	16½	17	17½
Japanese Size	36	37	38	39	40	41	42	43

HOKA NO YŌFUKU (OTHER CLOTHING)

American Size	34	36	38	40	42	44	46	48
Japanese Size	85	90	95	100	105	110	115	120
	S		M		L		LL	

If you are a man, what size shirt do you wear?

Watakushi wa, saizu ga ____ no waishatsu o kimasu.

What size suit do you wear?

Watakushi wa, saizu ga ____ no sūtsu o kimasu.

If you are a woman, what are the sizes of a male friend or relative?

Kare wa, saizu ga ____ no waishatsu to, saizu ga ____ no sūtsu o kimasu.

Fill in the blanks with the words depicted:

1. Samui toki wa, _____ o kimasu.

2. Samui toki wa, _____ o kimasu.

3. Yuki no toki wa, _____ o hakimasu.

4. Ame no toki wa, _____ o kimasu.

5. Ame no toki wa, _____ o tsukaimasu.

6. Atsui toki wa, _____ o hakimasu.

(shoh-tsoo)
shōtsu
shorts

145

FUJIN FUKU

Women's Clothes

(kee-hon   teh-kee   nah) (ee-roh)

Kihon teki na iro

Basic colors

(kee-roh-ee) (boo-rah-jah)

kiiroi   burajā

yellow bra

(shee-roh-ee) (soo-reep-poo)

shiroi   surippu

white slip

(koo-roh-ee) (hahn-doh-bahg-goo)

kuroi   handobaggu

black purse

(ah-oh-ee) (doh-reh-soo)

aoi   doresu

blue dress

(kee-roh-ee) (pahn-tee)

kiiroi   pantī

yellow panties

(mee-doh-ree ee-roh noh) (boo-rah-oo-soo)

midori iro no   burausu

green blouse

(ah-kah-ee) (skah-toh)

akai   sukāto

red skirt

(kee-roh) (koo-roh) (skah-foo)

kiiro to kuro no sukāfu

yellow and black scarf

Can you answer these questions?

Example: What color is the skirt? The skirt is red.

Sukāto wa, nani iro desu ka. Sukāto wa, akai desu.

1. Handobaggu wa, nani iro desu ka. _____.

2. Doresu wa, nani iro desu ka. _____.

Continue by asking and answering similar questions about the remaining items of clothing above.

(foo-jeen foo-koo) (noh) (sah-ee-zoo)

Fujin fuku no saizu

Women's Clothing Sizes

American Size	6	8	10	12	14	16
Japanese Size	5/7	7/9	9/11	11/13	13/15	15/17
	S	S	M	ML	LL	LL

ANSWERS

Colors 1. Handobaggu wa, kuroi desu. 2. Doresu wa, aoi desu.

DANSEI TO JOSEI NO KUTSU

(dahn-seh) *(joh-seh)* *(ktsoo)*

Shoes for Men and Women

Few Japanese shoes fit western feet. EE is the standard width, and large shoes are hard to find. If you do decide to brave a Japanese shoe store, don't rely only on the size chart. They tend to be inconsistent. Let the salesperson measure your feet.

(seh-mah-soo-gee)
Semasugi desu.
They're too narrow for me.

(oh-kee-soo-gee)
Ōkisugi desu.
They're too big for me.

(kee-tsoo-ee)
Kitsui desu.
They pinch my feet.

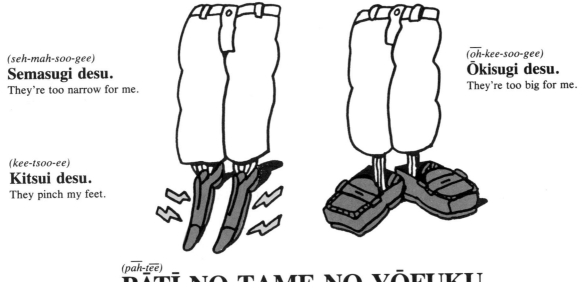

PĀTĪ NO TAME NO YŌFUKU

(pah-tee)

Clothes for the Party

Here's a story about Mary's adventures with clothing.

Merī san wa, pātī no tame
(ah-tah-rah-shee)(ee-roo-ee)
ni, atarashii irui ga irimasu.
(deh-pah-toh)
Kanojo wa, depāto e ikimasu.
(joh tehn-een)
Jo ten-in ga, tasukete kuremasu.

Kanojo wa, doresu o takusan

tameshimasu. Ōkii no mo, chiisai
(sah-ee-goh)
no mo arimasu. Saigo ni, kanojo

wa akai burausu to aoi sukāto o
(soh-reh-rah)
kaimasu. Sorera wa, pittari

aimasu.

Mary needs a new outfit for the party. She goes

to a department store. The saleswoman helps her.

She tries on many dresses. Some are too big, and

some are too small. Finally, she buys a red blouse

and a blue skirt. They fit perfectly.

(ktsoo

Tsugi ni Merī san wa, kutsu

oo-ree-bah)   *(oh-toh-koh)*

uriba e ikimasu. Otoko no

ten-in ga, tasukete kuremasu.

(nahn-soh-koo)

Kutsu o nansoku mo tameshimasu.

(doh-reh moh)

Keredomo dore mo aimasen.

Kanojo wa, Nihon no kutsu ga

(hah-keh-mah-sehn)   *(foo-roo-ee)*

hakemasen. Kanojo wa, furui

kutsu o haite pātī e ikimasu.

Pātī de Merī san wa,

Matsushima Yōko san ga onaji

yōfuku o kite iru no ni,

(kee-zoo-kee-mahs)

kizukimasu. Merī san wa, uchi

(kah-eht-teh)

ni kaette hoka no yōfuku o kiru

(beh-kee)

beki desu ka. Soretomo

(shoo-mee)

Matsushima san no ii shumi o

(hoh-meh-roo)

homeru beki desu ka.

Next, she goes to the shoe department. The salesman waits on her. She tries on many pairs of shoes, but nothing fits. She can't wear Japanese shoes. She'll wear her old shoes to the party.

At the party, she finds that Yoko Matsushima has on the same clothes as she does. Should she go home and put on other clothes? Or should she congratulate Ms. Matsushima on her good taste?

Here are some more clothing words and phrases to help you with your shopping in Japan:

I want something in _____ .

_____ **no mono ga hoshii desu.**

(nah-ee-rohn)	*(moh-mehn)*	*(kah-wah)*	*(deh-nee-moo)*	*(kee-noo)*	*(wōō-roo)*
nairon	**momen**	**kawa**	**denimu**	**kinu**	**wūru**
nylon	cotton	leather	denim	silk	wool

(soon-pōh)   *(hah-kaht-teh)*

Sunpō o hakatte kudasai.

Please take my measurements.

Mō sukoshi ii mono ga hoshii

no desu ga.

I'd like something of better quality.

148

(teh-zoo-koo-ree)
Nanika tezukuri no mono ga   Do you have something handmade?

 arimasu ka.

(nah-gah-soo-gee)
Nagasugi desu.   It's too *long* for me.

  (mee-jee-kah) **(chēe-sah)**
 (ōkisugi, mijikasugi, chiisasugi) (big, short, small)

Kono iro wa, suki dewa   I don't like the color. I prefer green.

 arimasen. Midori iro no
(hōh)
hō ga suki desu.

   (tah-meh-shteh-moh)
Sore o tameshitemo ii desu ka.   May I try it on?

Now have fun with the following crossword puzzle.

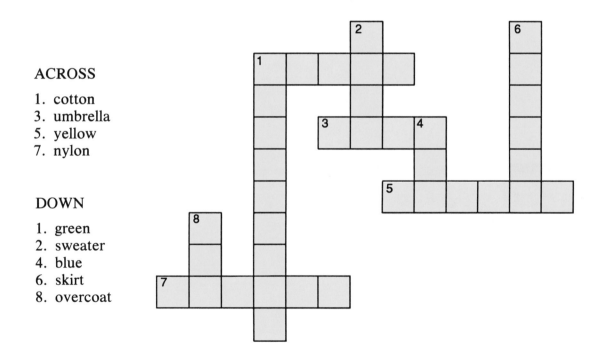

ACROSS

1. cotton
3. umbrella
5. yellow
7. nylon

DOWN

1. green
2. sweater
4. blue
6. skirt
8. overcoat

Shopping for food can be another pleasurable experience during your stay in Japan. Here are some helpful words.

(gyōō-nyōō) **gyūnyū ya** dairy (nee-koo) **niku ya** butcher shop (yah-sah-ee) **yasai ya** vegetable store (koo-dah-moh-noh) **kudamono ya** fruit store (pahn) **pan ya** bakery

gyūnyū milk **niku** meat **yasai** vegetables **kudamono** fruit **pan** bread

(sah-kah-nah) **sakana ya** fish store (oh-kah-shee) **okashi ya** candy store (keh-kee) **kēki ya** pastry shop (ah-ee-skoo-rēē-moo) **aisukurīmu ya** ice cream shop (sah-kah-yah) **sakaya** liquor store

sakana fish **okashi** candy **kēki** cake **aisukurīmu** ice cream (bēē-roo) (sah-keh) **bīru, sake** beer, sake

Now that you've studied the vocabulary, you can see that adding **ya** after the name of the food gives you the name of the shop. (Note that in **sakaya**, liquor store, the **ya** is attached.)
Ya *can't be used alone.* To say, "store," use the word **mise**.

Ōsugiru shitsumon
(oh-soo-gee-roo) (shee-tsoo-mohn)

Too many questions

Mark Smith and his wife, Mary, approach a policeman.

MARK **Chotto, sumimasen ga.**
(shteh-moh)
Shitsumon shitemo ii desu ka.

Excuse me, sir. I would like to ask you a question.

POLICEMAN **Dōzo.**

Go ahead.

MARK **Pan ga, irimasu. Pan ya wa, doko desu ka.**

I need some bread. Where is the bakery?

POLICEMAN *(meh-goo-roh doh-ree)* **Meguro Dōri no chikaku desu.**

Nearby on Meguro Dori.

MARK **Niku wa, doko de kaimasu ka.**

Where does one buy meat?

POLICEMAN **Niku ya de kaimasu.**

At the butcher shop.

MARK **Gyūnyū wa.**

And milk?

POLICEMAN **Gyūnyū ya desu.**

At the dairy.

MARK **Sorekara, yasai to kudamono mo irimasu. Ichiban** *(chee-kah-ee)* **chikai mise ga doko ka, oshiete kudasai.**

Then I also need vegetables and fruit. Can you tell me where the nearest market is?

POLICEMAN *(tah-ee-rah mah-chee) (shoh-tehn)* **Taira Machi Shōten** *(gah-ee)* **Gai desu.**

On Taira Machi Shoten Gai.

MARK **Sakana o sukoshi,** *(choh-koh-reh-toh)* **chokorēto o hito hako, kēki,**

I also need a little fish, a box of chocolates, a cake, and two bottles of wine. Can you tell me

(wah-een)
wain ga ni hon irimasu.

Sakana ya to, okashi ya to,

kēki ya to, sakaya o, doko de
(mee-tsoo-keh-roo)
mitsukeru ka oshiete kudasai.

MARY   **Māku, onegai. Shitsumon**
(oh-soo-gee-mahs)
ga ōsugimasu.

                (kah-mah-ee-mah-sehn)
POLICEMAN   **Iie, kamaimasen.**

Watakushi to issho ni
(ee-rahs-shah-ee)   *(tsoo-reh-teh)*
irasshai. Mise ni tsurete
(eet-teh)   *(ah-geh-mahs)*
itte   agemasu yo.

      (nahn-teh)   *(sheen-seh-tsoo)*
MARY   **Nante   shinsetsu na**
(oh-mah-wah-ree-sahn)
omawarisan deshō.

where to find a fish market, a candy store, a pastry shop, and a liquor store?

Mark, please! You're asking too many questions.

No, it's all right. Come with me. I'll take you to the stores.

What a kind policeman!

Write true or false next to these statements based on the dialogue.

1. Māku san wa, omawarisan ni shitsumon shitai desu.   1. _____

2. Māku san wa, pan ga irimasen.   2. _____

3. Niku wa, niku ya de kaimasu.   3. _____

4. Gyūnyū wa, gyūnyū ya de kaimasu.   4. _____

5. Yasai wa, aisukurīmu ya de kaimasu.   5. _____

6. Sakana wa, sakana ya de kaimasu.   6. _____

7. Wain wa, okashi ya de kaimasu.   7. _____

8. Omawarisan wa, totemo shinsetsu desu.   8. _____

ANSWERS

True-false 1. True **2.** False **3.** True **4.** True **5.** False **6.** True **7.** False **8.** True

152

MEKATA TO BUNRYŌ

(meh-kah-tah) *(boon-ryoh)*

Weights and Measures

(hah-kah-roo)

mekata o hakaru

to weigh

Although it hasn't yet caught on in the United States, the metric system is the standard means for measuring in many other countries. Here are some common weights and measures.

ENGLISH	JAPANESE	EQUIVALENT
100 grams	*(goo-rah-moo)* **hyaku guramu**	3.5 ounces (a little less than ¼ pound)
500 grams	**go hyaku guramu**	17.5 ounces (1 pound + 1.5 ounces)
1 kilo	*(kee-roh)* **ichi kiro**	2.2 pounds
1 milliliter	*(mee-ree-reet-toh-roo)* **ichi miririttoru**	0.034 liquid ounces
1 liter	*(reet-toh-roo)* **ichi rittoru**	1.06 quarts

Here are some useful expressions when buying food. Try writing them out:

(dāh-soo)

ichi dāsu   a dozen _____

han dāsu   a half dozen _____

ichi kiro   a kilo _____

go hyaku guramu   500 grams _____

ichi rittoru   a liter _____

Mekata wa dono kurai desu ka. How much does it weigh? _____

_____

Ōsugimasu.   It's too much. _____

Ichi dāsu ni tsuki ikura desu ka. How much are they per dozen? ___

_____

Ikura desu ka.

How much does it/do they cost? _____

_____

(tah-kah-soo-gee-mahs)
Takasugimasu.

It's too expensive. _____

(shoh-koo-ryōh-heen   *tehn)*
SHOKURYŌHIN TEN DE
At the Grocery Store

(toh-ee-reht-toh pēh-pāh) *(hee-toh)* *(mah-kee)*
toiretto pēpā hito maki
a roll of toilet paper

(sah-koo-rahn-boh) *(hah-kah-ree)*
sakuranbo o hakari de hakaru
weighing cherries on a scale

(een-stahn-toh kōh-hēē) *(been)*
insutanto kōhī hito bin
a jar of instant coffee

sakuranbo go hyaku guramu
500 grams of cherries

(kook-kēē)
kukkī hito hako
a box of cookies

(sehk-kehn)
sekken ikko
a bar of soap

(tah-mah-goh)
tamago hito hako
*a box of eggs

(sah-tōh)
satō ichi kiro
a kilo of sugar

    * Japanese buy eggs by the box of ten—not a dozen. In fact, the Japanese rarely use a unit of 12 for buying things. The most common things ordered by the dozen are pencils and golf balls, not food items. The Japanese do have the concept of a dozen, however, so if you use it, it will be understood.

Ask the clerk how much the items in the pictures cost.

1. Gyūnyū o ichi rittoru kudasai.

_____ ikura desu ka.

2. Remon o muttsu kudasai.

_____ ikura desu ka.

3. Instanto kōhī o hito bin kudasai.

_____ ikura desu ka.

4. Tamago o hito hako kudasai.

_____ ikura desu ka.

5. Sekken o ikko kudasai.

_____ ikura desu ka.

Nowadays, it isn't necessary to go to different stores to buy groceries in Japan. If you like, you can go to a large, modern supermarket and buy everything in one place.

In the cities, you may also want to look around the indoor food arcades. Often located near the train station, these arcades have many tiny shops offering both fresh food and cooked items.

In small cities and towns, you can find open air markets where farmers come to sell their local produce. It's a good way to see the typical foods of the region.

Japanese-style pharmacies are quite different from American drugstores. Most have only Japanese medicines and personal care products. You can find Western cosmetics, toiletries, and medicines in drugstores in the arcades of most major hotels. The drugstore staff can tell you where you can have a prescription filled. Take a supply of your prescription medicines with you to Japan as they may not be available there.

DORAGGUSUTOĀ DE
At the Drugstore

(hah-MEE-gah-kee)
hamigaki
toothpaste

(hah-BOO-rah-shee)
haburashi
toothbrush

(tees-shōō) *(hee-toh hah-koh)*
tisshū   hito hako
box of tissues

(koo-chee-beh-nee)
kuchibeni
lipstick

(kōh-roo-doh koo-rēē-moo)
kōrudo kurīmu
face cream

(ahn-zehn peen)
anzen pin
safety pins

(heh-āh boo-rah-shee)
heā burashi
hairbrush

(kah-gah-mee)
kagami
mirror

(koo-shee)
kushi
comb

(heh-āh spoo-rēh)
heā supurē
hairspray

(mah-nee-kyoo-ah)
manikyua
nail polish

Mary Smith and Yuko Inoue, a Japanese friend, are at a drugstore.

MARY *(koo-rehn-jeen-goo koo-rēē-moo)* **Kurenjingu kurīmu to tisshū ga hito hako irimasu.**

I need some cleansing cream and a box of tissues.

MS. INOUE **Sore dake desu ka.**

Is that all?

MARY **Iie, hoka ni mo sukoshi irimasu.**

No. I need a few more things, too.

MS. INOUE **Merī san, ki o** *(kee tskeh-teh)* **tsukete.** *(deh-wah)* **Koko dewa,** *(oh-moht-tah)* **omotta** *(yoh-ree)* **yori mono ga takai desu yo.**

Be careful, Mary. These things are more expensive here than you think.

MARY **Shinpai shinai de. Daijōbu desu.**

Don't worry. It's okay.

CLERK **Nanika, goiriyō desu ka.**

May I help you?

MARY **Kushi to, heā burashi to, heā supurē ga irimasu. Sore** *(soh-reh nee)* **ni, haburashi to hamigaki mo onegai shimasu.**

I need a comb, a hair brush, and a can of hair spray. I'd also like to buy a toothbrush and toothpaste.

MS. INOUE *(sah-sah-yah-ee-teh)* **(sasayaite) Merī san, watakushi ga itta koto oboete imasu ka.**

(whispering) Do you remember what I told you, Mary?

(oh-keh-shoh heen) MARY **Hai. *Okeshō hin mo**	Yes. Now I'd like to see the cosmetics. Lipstick,
mitai desu. Kuchibeni to, *(hoh-oh-beh-nee)* *(mahs-kah-rah)* **hoobeni to, masukara o onegai** *(ah soh-reh-kah-rah)* **shimasu. Ā sorekara,**	blusher, and mascara, please. Oh, yes, nail polish and nail polish remover, too.
(joh-koh-eh-kee) **manikyua to jokōeki mo misete** **kudasai.**	
(oh-kah-neh) MS. INOUE **Merī san, okane no** *(tskah-ee-soo-gee)* **tsukaisugi desu yo.**	Mary, you're spending too much!
MARY **Ee, wakatte imasu.** **Keredomo, korera wa hitsuyō** **desu.**	Yes, I know. But I need these things.

*Here's an example of the polite **o** that Japanese women use at the beginning of some words. In
(keh-shoh heen)
Japanese, "cosmetics" is **keshō hin.** When women say it, they usually precede it with **o.**

   True or false? Choose the correct answer.

1. Merī san wa, doraggusutoā de nanika irimasu.   1. _____

2. Inoue san wa, sorera wa takai kara ki o tsukeru yō ni iimasu.   2. _____

3. Merī san wa, kushi to, heā burashi to, heā supurē o kaimasu.   3. _____

4. Kanojo wa, haburashi to hamigaki o kaimasen.   4. _____
   (mee-tah-koo)
5. Kanojo wa, keshō hin o mitaku arimasen.   5. _____
   doesn't want to see

ANSWERS

True-false 1. True 2. True 3. True 4. False 5. False

158

Atarashii dōshi

New verbs

iu		
to say, to tell		
	AFFIRMATIVE	NEGATIVE
PRESENT	*(ee-mahs)* **iimasu**	*(ee-mah-sehn)* **iimasen**
PRESENT CONTINUOUS	*(eet-teh)* **itte imasu**	**itte imasen**
PAST	*(ee-mahsh-tah)* **iimashita**	**iimasen deshita**

(mee-seh-roo) **miseru**		
to show		
	AFFIRMATIVE	NEGATIVE
PRESENT	*(mee-seh-mahs)* **misemasu**	*(mee-seh-mah-sehn)* **misemasen**
PRESENT CONTINUOUS	*(mee-seh-teh)* **misete imasu**	**misete imasen**
PAST	*(mee-seh-mahsh-tah)* **misemashita**	**misemasen deshita**

Write the name of the item on the line provided.

(tah-bah-koh)
tabako
cigarettes

(rah-ee-tāh)
raitā
lighter

(spoo-reh)   *(deh-oh-doh-rahn-toh)*
supurē no deodoranto
deodorant spray

(dehn-kee   kah-mee-soh-ree)
denki   kamisori
electric razor

(kah-mee-soh-ree)
kamisori
razor

(hah)
kamisori no ha
razor blades

Mark Smith and Kenji Shimura, a Japanese friend, are at a drugstore.

MARK   **Koko de, nanika kau hitsuyō ga arimasu ka.**

Do you need to buy anything here?

MR. SHIMURA   **Iie. Tabako ga irimasu ga, doraggustoā dewa** *(oot-teh)* **utte imasen. Anata wa dō desu ka.**

No. I need some cigarettes, but they're not sold in a drugstore. How about you?

MARK   **Watakushi wa, deodoranto ga irimasu. Sorekara kamisori no ha mo irimasu.**

I need some deodorant. And a razor and some blades.

MR. SHIMURA   **Denki kamisori wa** *(moht-teh ee-nah-ee)* **motte inai no desu ka.**

Don't you have an electric razor?

MARK   **Motte imasu. Keredomo** *(dehn-ah-tsoo)* *(chee-gah-oo)* **denatsu ga chigau no dewa arimasen ka.**

Yes, I do. But isn't the voltage different here?

MR. SHIMURA   *(skoh-shee)* **Sukoshi chigaimasu.** *(boh-roo-toh)* **100 boruto desu.**

Koko de, anata no denki *(tskah-eh-mahs)* **kamisori o tsukaemasu yo.** *(heh-āh doh-rah-ee-yāh)* **Heā doraiyā mo daijōbu desu.**

It's slightly different. 100 volts. You can use your electric razor here. And a hair dryer too.

MARK   **Sore wa subarashii.**

Anata ga, kamisori to *(dah-ee-keen)* **kamisori no ha no daikin o** *(seh-tsoo-yah-koo)* *(koo-reh-mahsh-tah)* **setsuyaku shite kuremashita.**

Wonderful. You saved me the price of a razor and blades!

1. Name something you *don't* find in a drugstore. _____

2. What do you put inside a razor? _____

3. What is the voltage in Japan? _____

Here are some more useful phrases for buying things at a drugstore. Write the name of each of the items on the line indicated:

(ahs-pee-reen)
asupirin
aspirin

_____

(oh-moo-tsoo)
omutsu
diapers

_____

(sheek-kah-rōh-roo)
shikkarōru
talcum powder

_____

(bahn-sōh-kōh)
bansōkō
adhesive bandage

_____

(tah-ee-ohn-kēh)
taionkei
thermometer

_____

(ahn-zehn peen)
anzen pin
safety pins

_____

Now read about Mary's trip to the drugstore with her friend.

(nahn-shēē
Merī san to tomodachi no Nanshī
pāh-keen-soo)   *(kah-ee-moh-noh)*
Pākinsu san wa, sukoshi kaimono

suru tame ni, doraggusutoā e

ikimasu. Merī san wa, bansōkō
(yah-koo-yōh ah-roo-kōh-roo)
to, yakuyō   arukōru to, taionkei

o tanomimasu. Merī san wa
(tehn-een)   *(zoo-tsōō)*
ten-in ni zutsū ga suru to itte,

asupirin mo tanomimasu.
(neen-sheen chōō)
Ninshin chū no Nanshī san wa,

shikkaroru to, anzen pin

to, omutsu o tanomimasu.

Mary and her friend, Nancy Perkins, go into the drugstore to buy a few things. Mary asks for adhesive bandages, rubbing alcohol, and a thermometer. She tells the clerk she has a headache, and she also asks for aspirin.

Nancy, who is pregnant, asks for talcum powder, safety pins, and diapers.

161

(ah-kah-chahn)　　*(oo-mah-reh-roo)*　*(yoh-teh)*
"Akachan wa, itsu umareru　yotei
　　　　　(toh)
desu ka" to Merī san ga
　　　　(ee-tsoo deh-moh)
kikimasu. "Itsu demo" to
　　　　　　(koh-tah-eh-mahs)
Nanshī san ga kotaemasu. "Koko

ni, isu ga arimasu. Dōzo
(oh-kah-keh)
okake kudasai," to ten-in ga

iimasu.

"When is your baby due?" Mary asks. "Any time now," Nancy replies. "Here's a chair. Please sit down," says the clerk.

If you're sick and need some over-the-counter medicine, these sentences and phrases will help.

In English, to describe an illness or a symptom, you just say, "I have . . ." and fill in the symptom: a cough, a fever, a headache.

Japanese has different structures for different symptoms. Here are some sentences you may need:

diarrhea	*(geh-ree)* **Geri** o shite imasu.	I have diarrhea.
diabetes	*(toh-nyoh-byoh)* **Tōnyōbyō** desu.	I have diabetes.
a cough	*(seh-kee)* **Seki** ga demasu.	I have a cough.
a fever	*(neh-tsoo)* **Netsu** ga arimasu.	I have a fever.
cramps, a stomachache	*(oh-nah-kah)(ee-tah-ee)* **Onaka ga itai** desu.	I have a stomachache.
a headache	*(ah-tah-mah)(ee-tah-ee)* **Atama ga itai** desu./ **Zutsū** ga shimasu.	I have a headache.
a cut	*(kee-ree-kee-zoo)* **Kirikizu** desu.	I have a cut.
a sunburn	*(hee-yah-keh)* **Hiyake** desu.	I have a sunburn.
the flu	*(ryoo-kahn)* **Ryūkan** desu.	I have the flu.

| a toothache | *(hah)* *(ee-tah-ee)*
Ha ga itai desu. | I have a toothache. |
| constipation | *(behn-pee)*
Benpi desu. | I'm constipated. |

To ask for items you need, you can use one of the structures you've already learned:

. . . . **o kudasai.**   give me (please)
. . . . **o onegai shimasu.**   please
. . . . **ga irimasu.**   (I need)

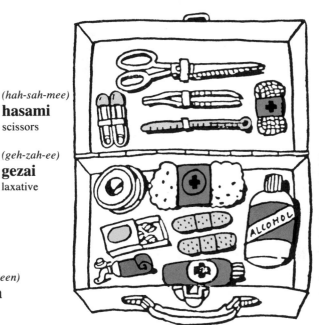

(tahn-pohn) **tanpon** tampons	*(hah-sah-mee)* **hasami** scissors	*(yōh-doh-cheen-kee)* **yōdochinki** iodine	
(ee-sahn) **isan** antacid	*(geh-zah-ee)* **gezai** laxative	*(hōh-tah-ee)* **hōtai** bandages	*(shōh-dohk-yah-koo)* **shōdokuyaku** antiseptic
(dahs-shee-mehn) **dasshimen** cotton		*(een-shoo-reen)* **inshurin** insulin	
(sēh-ree nah-poo-keen) **seiri napukin** sanitary napkins		*(seh-kee-doh-meh shee-rohp-poo)* **sekidome shiroppu** cough syrup	

Match the ailment (column 1) with the item or items (column 2) you would most likely ask for at the drugstore or pharmacy. Sometimes more than one answer may be possible.

_____ 1. netsu	a. sekidome shiroppu
_____ 2. kirikizu	b. shōdokuyaku
_____ 3. onaka ga itai	c. asupirin
_____ 4. seki	d. isan
_____ 5. atama ga itai	e. hōtai
_____ 6. benpi	f. gezai
	g. taionkei
	h. yōdochinki

Major tourist hotels in Japan provide the normal range of laundry and dry cleaning services. You can find outside laundries and dry cleaners as well. The services are good, although dry cleaning may take longer than you're used to. Laundromats are available too, though not so many as you find in the United States.

(sehn-tah-koo kee)
sentaku ki
washing machine

(kahn-sōh kee)
kansō ki
dryer

(koh-nah sehk-kehn hee-toh hah-koh)
kona sekken hito hako
box of soap powder

(ah-ee-rohn dah-ee)
airon dai
ironing board

(ah-ee-rohn)
airon
iron

(sehn-tah-koo bah-sah-mee)
sentaku basami
clothes pins

(sehn-tah-koo kah-goh)
sentaku kago
laundry basket

HOTERU NO SENTAKU TO
(sah-bee-soo)
DORAIKURĪNINGU NO SĀBISU
Hotel Laundry and Dry Cleaning Services

Since you may not want to spend time in laundromats in Japan, you will probably use the laundry services of the hotels where you stay. These expressions may be useful.

Sentaku no sābisu ga, arimasu ka. — Do you have a laundry service?

(sehn-tah-koo moh-noh)
Sentaku mono ga arimasu. — I have some clothes to be washed.

(boh-tahn) *(tskeh-teh)*
Kore ni, botan o tsukete moraemasu ka. — Can you sew on this button?

(soh-deh) *(nah-oh-shteh)*
Sode o, naoshite moraemasu ka. — Can you mend the sleeve?

(noh-ree) *(kah-keh-nah-ee-deh)*
Waishatsu niwa, nori o kakenaide kudasai. — I don't want any starch in my shirts.

Waishatsu ni, karuku nori o *(kah-roo-koo)*

kakete kudasai. *(kah-keh-teh)*

I want light starch in my shirts.

Kono waishatsu ni mō ichido *(mōh ee-chee-doh)*

airon o kakete kudasai.

Please iron this shirt again.

Kono sūtsu o, dorai kurīningu *(sōo-tsoo)*

shite moraemasu ka.

Could you have this suit dry cleaned?

Kono shimi o, nuite moraemasu *(shee-mee) (noo-ee-teh)*

ka.

Can you take out this spot?

Try filling in the blanks with the key words from the sentences above. Then read the sentences aloud.

1. Kono sūtsu o, _____ moraemasu ka.
   dry cleaned

2. _____ niwa, nori o kakenaide kudasai.
   shirts

3. Kono _____ o, nuite moraemasu ka.
   spot

4. _____ ga arimasu ka.
   A laundry service

5. Waishatsu ni, karuku _____ o kakete kudasai.
   starch

6. Kono waishatsu ni mō ichido _____ o kakete kudasai.
   iron

7. _____ o, naoshite moraemasu ka.
   sleeve

8. _____ ga arimasu.
   clothes to be washed

9. Kore ni, _____ o tsukete moraemasu ka.
   button

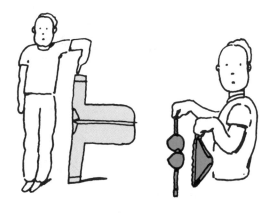

Māku san wa, itsumo yōfuku o

hoteru no sentaku no sābisu ni
(dah-shee-mahs) (foo-tsōō) (shee-ah-gah-ree)
dashimasu. Futsū, shiagari wa
(kohn-doh)
subarashii desu. Keredomo kondo
(mohn-dah-ee) *(mah-chee-gah-ee)*
wa, mondai ga arimasu. Machigai
(aht-teh)
ga atte, hoka no hito no yōfuku
(moh-doht-teh kee-mahs)
ga, Māku san ni, modotte kimasu.
(mah-nēh-jah)
Māku san wa, manējā ni kujō o
(dah-ee ee-chee)
iimasu. Dai ichi, Māku san wa

josei no shitagi wa kimasen.
(soh-noh-oo-eh)
Sonoue, waishatsu wa nori ga
(kee-kee-soo-gee-teh)
kikisugite imasu. Ichi mai no

waishatsu wa,
(dah-ee-nah-shee nee naht-teh)
dainashi ni natte shimaimashita.
(koh-geh-meh   tsoo-ee-teh)
Kogeme ga tsuite iru kara desu.
(mah-tah)(koo-tsoo-shtah)   (ah-kah)
Mata, kutsushita ga ni mai, aka

ga ichi mai, midori ga ichi mai,

Mark always sends his clothes to the hotel

laundry service. They usually do an excellent job.

This time there are problems. There is a mix-up,

and many of the clothes they return to him belong

to another person.

He complains to the manager. In the first place,

he never wears women's underwear. Besides, his

shirts have too much starch in them, and one is

ruined; it's scorched. Also, he is missing two

socks, one red and one green. The suit he

receives from the cleaner's still has a spot on the

sleeve. He has reason to complain, don't you

think?

(nah-koo-naht-teh)
nakunatte imasu. Kurīningu
(oo-keh-toht-tah)
kara ukettota sūtsu wa, mada
(tsoo-ee-teh)
sode ni shimi ga tsuite imasu.

Māku san niwa, kujō o iu riyū

ga arimasu. Sō omoimasen ka.

True or false? Choose the correct answer.

1. Māku san wa, itsumo yōfuku o hoteru no sentaku no sābisu ni dashimasu.　1. _____

2. Māku san wa, manējā ni kujō o iimasen.　2. _____

3. Māku san wa, josei no shitagi wa kimasen.　3. _____

Here are some phrases to use if you have a complaint.

Kujō ga arimasu.   I have a complaint.

(mah-chee-gah-ee)
Machigai ga arimasu.   There's a mistake.

(hoh-kah noh hee-toh
Kono yōfuku wa, hoka no hito   These clothes belong to somebody else.
noh)
no desu.

Kono waishatsu wa, nori ga   This shirt has too much starch.

kikisugite imasu.

Watakushi no yōfuku wa,   My clothes are ruined.

dainashi ni natte shimaimashita.

Kono waishatsu wa, kogeme ga   This shirt is scorched.

tsuite imasu.

167

Botan ga nakunatte imasu.

There's a button missing.

Kono zubon niwa, shimi ga

arimasu.

There's a spot on these trousers.

(ees-soh-koo)
Kutsushita ga issoku, nakunatte

I'm missing a pair of socks.

imasu.

A note of caution: if you have a complaint about something, express it gently. In Japan, a loud voice or an accusatory tone may compound rather than solve a problem. A calm, polite manner is more appropriate.

(bee-yōh-een)
Biyōin
The Beauty Shop/The Hairdresser

(heh-āh sah-rohn)
Heā saron
The Hair Stylist/Salon

(toh-koh-yah)
Tokoya
The Barber Shop

BIYŌIN DE
At the Beauty Shop/Hairdresser

(kah-mee-noh-keh)
kaminoke
hair

(nah-gah-ee)
nagai
long

(mee-jee-kah-ee)
mijikai
short

(chah-ee-roh noh)
chairo no
brown

(keen-pah-tsoo noh)
kinpatsu no
blond

(shahn-pōo)
shanpū
shampoo

(boo-rah-shee)
burashi
brush

(boo-rah-shee oh kah-keh-roo)
burashi o kakeru
to brush

(heh-āh doh-rah-ee-yāh)
heā doraiyā
hair dryer

(pāh-mah-nehn-toh)
pāmanento
permanent

(mah-nee-kyoo-ah)
manikyua
manicure

(kāh-rāh)
kārā
rollers

(bee-gahn-joo-tsoo)
biganjutsu
facial massage

Mary and Anne decide to go to a beauty shop.

(ee-rahs-shah-ee-mah-seh)

HAIRSTYLIST **Irasshaimase.**　　　　May I help you?

(kaht-toh) *(boo-rōh*

ANNE **Shanpū to, katto to, burō**　　　I'd like a shampoo, cut, and blow dry.

doh-rah-ee)
dorai o onegai shimasu.

HAIRSTYLIST **Wakarimashita.**	I see. And you, Madame?
(ohk-sah-mah)	
Okusama wa.	
(seht-toh)	
MARY **Shanpū to, setto to,**	I want a shampoo, set, and manicure.
manikyua o onegai shimasu.	
HAIRSTYLIST **Katto wa**	You don't want me to cut your hair?
(yoh-roh-shēē)	
shinakute yoroshii desu ka.	
MARY **Kekkō desu.**	No thank you.
HAIRSTYLIST **(kanojo no kami-**	(washing her hair) How about a permanent? Or
(ah-rah-ee-nah-gah-rah)	
noke o arainagara)	perhaps a color rinse?
(ee-kah-gah)	
Pāmanento wa ikaga desu ka.	
(kah-rāh reen-soo)	
Soretomo kara rinsu wa.	
MARY **Kyō wa kekkō desu.**	No, not today. I like my hair color.
(heh-āh kah-rāh)	
Watakushi wa kono heā karā	
ga suki desu.	
(doh-rah-ee-yāh)	
HAIRSTYLIST **Hai, doraiyā e**	Okay, you're ready to go under the dryer now.
(joon-bee) (deh-kee-mahsh-tah)	
iku junbi ga dekimashita.	
(oh-waht-tah)	
(Merī san ga owatta ato)	(after Mary is finished)
(goh-rahn	
HAIRSTYLIST **Kagami de, goran**	You can look at yourself in the mirror now.
nee naht-teh)	
ni natte kudasai.	
MARY **Arigatō gozaimashita.**	Thank you. It's wonderful.
Subarashii desu.	

Here are some more useful expressions:

Ashita no yoyaku o shitai no

desu ga.

I'd like an appointment for tomorrow.

Shanpū to katto o onegai

shimasu.

Could you wash and cut my hair?

Burō dorai o onegai shimasu.

Could you blow dry my hair?

(mah-eh-gah-mee)
Maegami o sagete kudasai.

I'd like bangs, please.

(mee-jee-kah-koo)
Mō sukoshi, mijikaku shite

kudasai.

A little shorter, please.

(mah-mah)
Soko wa nagai mama ni shite

kudasai.

Leave it long, please.

(tskah-wah-nah-ee-deh)
Heā supurē wa, tsukawanaide

kudasai.

Don't use any hairspray, please.

Now fill in the blanks with the words you have learned in this lesson.

1. _____ de, goran ni natte kudasai.
       mirror

2. _____ o onegai shimasu.
       blow dry

3. _____ to _____ o onegai shimasu.
       shampoo   cut

4. _____ o onegai shimasu.
       permanent

5. Mō sukoshi, _____ kudasai.
                  shorter

6. _____ wa, tsukawanaide kudasai.
       hairspray

HEĀ SARON/TOKOYA DE

At the Hairstylist/Barber

tokoya
barber

hasami
scissors

kamisori
straight razor

(bah-ree-kahn)
barikan
clippers

(hee-geh-soh-ree)
higesori
shave

(shēh-been-goo koo-rēē-moo)
shēbingu kurīmu
shaving cream

(hee-geh oh soh-roo)
hige o soru
to shave oneself

(toh-kah-shteh)
kaminoke o tokashite
to have one's hair combed

(moh-rah-oo)
morau

(toh-kah-soo)
kaminoke o tokasu
to comb one's own hair

(hee-geh) *(moh-mee-ah-geh)*
hige to momiage
beard and sideburns

(kah-ree-soh-roh-eh-roo)
karisoroeru
to trim

(sahn-pah-tsoo)
sanpatsu
haircut

(hah-geh ah-tah-mah)
hage atama
bald head

Need a haircut? You may be in for a pleasant surprise. In many places, a head, neck, and shoulder massage comes with it. If you color your hair, have it done *before* you go to Japan. Also, hairstylists in the tourist hotels are more expensive than local shops, but they're used to working with foreigners.

Henrī Jōnzu san wa, sanpatsu ga
(nah-noh-deh)
hitsuyō nanode, heā saron

e ikimasu. Hajime ni, shanpū o
(moh-rah-ee-mahs)
shite moraimasu. Itsumo
(nah-reh-teh-ee-roo)
nareteiru shanpū yori jikan ga
(kah-kah-ree-mahs)   *(bee-yoh-shee)*
kakarimasu. Sorekara biyōshi
(ah-tah-mah)   *(koo-bee)*
wa Jōnzu san no atama to, kubi
(kah-tah)   *(mahs-sah-jee)*
to, kata o massaji shimasu.

Kore mo, jikan ga kakarimasu.
(toh-teh-moh)
Jōnzu san wa, sore o totemo
(tah-noh-shee-mee-mahs)   *(jees-sah-ee)*
tanoshimimasu.   **Jissai, kare**
(neh-moot-teh shee-mah-ee-mahs)
wa isu de nemutte   **shimaimasu.**
(meh gah sah-meh-roo)
Jōnzu san wa me ga sameru to,

kagami o mimasu. Kare wa,

"Watakushi no kaminoke o dō
(chee-jee-reh-teh)
shita no desu ka. Chijirete
(sah-keh-bee-mahs)
imasu." to sakebimasu.

Biyōshi wa, "Pāmanento ga suki

dewa nai no desu ka. Nihon
(sah-ee-sheen noh)
dewa, kore ga saishin no
(fahs-shohn)
fasshon desu yo," to iimasu.

Henry Jones goes to the hairstylist because he

needs a haircut. First he has a shampoo. It lasts

much longer than he's used to. Then the

hairstylist massages his head, neck, and

shoulders. That, too, lasts a long time. He enjoys

it very much. In fact, he falls asleep in the chair!

When he wakes up, he looks in the mirror.

"What have you done to my hair? It's curly!" he

shouts. "Oh, don't you like the perm?" says the

hairstylist. "It's the latest fashion here in Japan!"

Try writing out these expressions, which could come in handy. Then read the sentences aloud.

Where is a good barber/hairstylist?

Jōzu na tokoya/heā saron wa, doko ni arimasu ka.

Whose turn is it now?
(doh-nah-tah) (bahn)
Donata no ban desu ka.

I need a haircut.

Sanpatsu shite kudasai.

I need a shave.

(soht-teh)
Hige o sotte kudasai.

No shave, please.

(soh-rah-nahk-teh)
Hige wa soranakute ii desu.

Long in back, short in front.

(nah-gah-koo)   (mee-jee-kah-koo)
Ushiro o nagaku, mae o mijikaku shite kudasai.

A little shorter here, please.

Soko o mō sukoshi, mijikaku shite kudasai.

That looks fine.

(kehk-kōh)
Kekkō desu.

How much do I owe you?

Ikahodo desu ka.

174

SHINBUN URIBA DE
At the Newsstand

English language newspapers from overseas are available at the newsstands in major hotels. Most Japanese newsstands, or kiosks, are located at train stations rather than on the street.

(zahs-shee)
zasshi
magazine

shinbun
newspaper

(eh-hah-gah-kee)
ehagaki
picture postcards

(keet-teh)
kitte
postage stamps

tabako
cigarettes

ANNE **Chotto sumimasen ga, eigo no shinbun ga arimasu ka.**

Excuse me, do you have English language newspapers?

CLERK **Hai. Nihon de** *(shoop-pahn-sah-reh-teh)* **shuppansarete iru, eigo no shinbun desu.**

Yes. We have English language newspapers that are published in Japan.

ANNE **Sore de ii desu. Kore o kudasai. Sorekara, ehagaki mo hoshii desu.**

Good. I'll take this one. I'd also like some picture postcards.

CLERK **Kore wa, Nihon no shuto,** *(shoo-toh)* **Tokyo no kirei na fūkei no** *(fōo-kēh)* **ehagaki desu.**

Here are some nice cards with views of Tokyo, our capital.

ANNE	**Kitte wa utte imasu ka.**	Do you sell postage stamps?

CLERK **Iie. Keredomo michi no**
(moo-koh-gah-wah) (mee-seh)
mukōgawa no mise ga utte
(oh-moh-jee)
imasu. Akai ōmoji no T no ue
(yoh-koh) (sehn) (yoh nah)
ni yoko   sen ga aru yō na sain
(mee-eh-mahs)
ga miemasu ka. Are ga, kitte
(koh-toh) (ee-mee-shee-mahs)
o utte iru koto o imishimasu.

No. But the shop across the street does. Do you see the sign that looks like a red capital T with a bar across the top? That means they sell stamps.

(doh dehs kah)
ANNE **Tabako wa dō desu ka.**

What about cigarettes?

(soo-goo)
CLERK **Tabako wa, sugu migi no**
(jee-doh hahn-bah-ee-kee)
jidō hanbaiki de kaemasu.

You can buy them in the vending machine just to your right.

ANNE **Wakarimashita. Shinbun to ehagaki wa, ikahodo desu ka.**

I see. How much do I owe you for the newspaper and postcards?

Match these Japanese words or phrases from the dialogue with their English equivalents:

1. shinbun
2. tabako
3. ehagaki
4. kitte

a. cigarettes
b. newspapers
c. stamps
d. picture postcards

176

BUNBŌGU TEN DE
At the Stationery Store

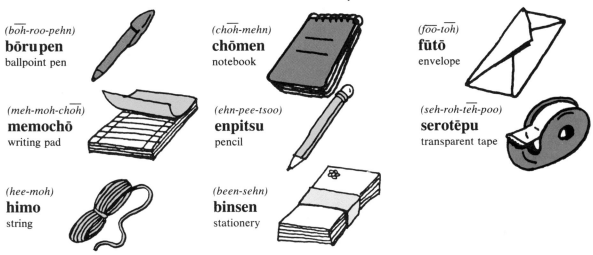

(bōh-roo-pehn)
bōrupen
ballpoint pen

(chōh-mehn)
chōmen
notebook

(foo-toh)
fūtō
envelope

(meh-moh-chōh)
memochō
writing pad

(ehn-pee-tsoo)
enpitsu
pencil

(seh-roh-teh-poo)
serotēpu
transparent tape

(hee-moh)
himo
string

(been-sehn)
binsen
stationery

Have you learned the new words well enough to recognize them all scrambled up? Try to straighten them out.

sitepnu _____   hnōemc _____   tōūf _____

ōemcmoh _____   tusorēpe _____   omih _____

nbnise _____   purōben _____

Futari no josei ga, bunbōgu ten

e ikimasu. Saisho no josei wa,

binsen to fūtō o kaimasu.
(nee-bahn-meh)
Nibanme no josei wa, bōrupen to,

memochō to, serotēpu o kaimasu.

Saisho no josei wa Amerikajin
(deh)
no kankō kyaku de, nibanme no
(ee-gee-ree-soo-jeen)
josei wa Igirisujin no kankō
(soh-noh-ah-toh)
kyaku desu. Sonoato, futari wa
(kees-sah-tehn)
kissaten e itte, kōhī o

nomimasu.

Two women enter a stationery store. The first woman buys some stationery and envelopes. The second buys a ballpoint pen, a writing pad, and some transparent tape. The first woman is an American tourist, the second one, an English tourist. Afterward, they go to a coffee shop to drink some coffee.

177

Choose the correct letter to answer each question.

1. Dare ga, bunbōgu ten e ikimasu ka.

   a. Igirisujin no josei ga futari.
   b. Amerikajin no josei ga futari.
   c. Amerikajin no josei ga hitori to, Igirisujin no josei ga hitori.

2. Dare ga, fūtō o kaimasu ka.

   a. Amerikajin no josei.
   b. Igirisujin no josei.
   (foo-rahn-soo-jeen)
   c. Furansujin no josei.

3. Dare ga, memochō o kaimasu ka.

   a. Amerikajin no josei.
   b. Igirisujin no josei.
   c. Furansujin no josei.

4. Futari no josei wa, doko e ikimasu ka.

   a. Eiga.
   (bāh)
   b. Bā.
   Bar
   c. Kissaten

Now let's end with a word puzzle. Find the following words: envelope, pencil, newspaper, cigarettes, stamps, magazines, stationery, picture postcards. One of the words is already circled for you.

K	P	O	J	O	E	D	B	U	K	A	S
L	F	Q	I	D	E	M	E	C	I	U	N
N	U	M	H	N	A	F	R	I	T	B	T
R	T	S	O	A	X	I	Q	Y	T	M	A
U	O	S	T	K	U	C	B	A	E	S	B
W	V	E	H	A	G	A	K	I	T	A	A
B	U	Q	I	U	G	O	Z	E	I	P	K
I	A	T	Z	A	S	S	H	I	D	I	O
N	F	O	I	F	E	T	G	S	U	R	Z
S	S	L	C	Z	J	A	E	I	F	A	P
E	X	T	O	E	N	P	I	T	S	U	L
N	B	L	O	X	S	H	I	N	B	U	N

178

HŌSHOKUTEN DE

At the Jewelry Store

(oo-deh-wah)
udewa
bracelet

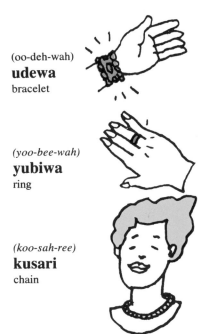

(nehk-koo-rehs)
nekkuresu
necklace

(boo-roh-chee)
burōchi
brooch

(yoo-bee-wah)
yubiwa
ring

(hoh-seh-kee ee-ree noh yoo-bee-wah)
hōseki iri no yubiwa
ring with stone

(koo-sah-ree)
kusari
chain

(ee-yah-reen-goo)
iyaringu
earrings

As Mark and Anne are looking around a jewelry store in Tokyo, a tall, handsome man enters.

CLERK **Irasshaimase.**

May I help you?

CUSTOMER **Tsuma ni, nanika** *(tah-boon)* **kaitai no desu ga. Tabun** *(sheen-joo)* **shinju no nekkuresu toka.**

I would like to buy something for my wife. A pearl necklace, perhaps.

CLERK **Koko ni, utsukushii** *(oo-tsoo-koo-shee)* *(sahn-rehn noh)* **sanren no shinju no nekkuresu ga gozaimasu.**

Here's a lovely 3-strand pearl necklace.

CUSTOMER **Kirei desu ne. Sore** *(ah-oo)* **o itadakimasu. Sore ni au iyaringu ga arimasu ka.**

It's pretty, isn't it? I'll take it. Do you have some earrings to match?

CLERK **Koko ni, nekkuresu ni**
  (soo-bah-rah-shee)
au subarashii iyaringu ga
  (keen)
gozaimasu. Kin ni, shinju ga
(hah-meh-kohn-deh)
hamekonde arimasu.

Here's an excellent pair to match. Pearls set in gold.

CUSTOMER **Sore mo itadakimasu.**

Kin no udewa wa arimasu ka.

I'll take them too. And do you have a gold bracelet?

  (ohk-sah-mah)
CLERK **Kore wa minna okusama**
(noh tah-meh)   *(oon gah ee)*
no tame desu ka. Un ga ii
(kah-tah)
kata desu ne.

Is all this for your wife, sir? She's a lucky person.

  (noh)
CUSTOMER **Un ga ii no wa,**

watakushi desu yo. Kore wa
  (nahn-dehs)
minna, tsuma no okane nandesu

kara.

I'm the lucky one. It's *her* money!

1. Name two items of jewelry you might wear on your fingers.

   _____ , _____

2. What jewelry do women wear on their ears?

   _____

3. What two items of jewelry are worn around the neck?

   _____ , _____

4. What is worn on the wrist? _____

5. What might a woman pin on her dress? _____

Practice writing the new words on the lines under the pictures.

(dah-ee-yah-mohn-doh)
daiyamondo
diamond

shinju
pearls

(sah-fah-ee-yah)
safaiya
sapphire

(eh-meh-rah-roo-doh)
emerarudo
emerald

(roo-bēē)
rubī
ruby

_____ _____ _____ _____ _____

(toh-pāh-zoo)
topāzu
topaz

(poo-rah-chee-nah)
purachina
platinum

(geen)
gin
silver

kin
gold

_____ _____ _____ _____

TOKEIYA DE
At the Watchmaker's Shop

(oo-deh-doh-kēh)
udedokei
wristwatch
_____

(meh-zah-mah-shee)
mezamashi
alarm clock
_____

tokeiya
watchmaker's shop _____

_____ **tokeiya**
watchmaker

Practice writing the new words by filling in the blanks under the pictures. Once you have done this, read aloud the sentences below. Then try writing them out in the spaces provided.

(toh-keh) (nah-oh-shteh)
Kono tokei o naoshite moraemasu ka.
Can you fix this watch?

_____

(soh-jee-shteh)
Tokei o sōjishite moraemasu ka.
Can you clean my watch?

_____

(soo-soo-mee-gah-chee)
Tokei ga susumigachi desu.
My watch is fast.

_____

(oh-koo-reh-gah-chee)
Mezamashi ga okuregachi desu.
My alarm clock is slow.

_____

(toh-maht-teh)
Tokei ga, tomatte shimaimashita.
My watch has stopped.

_____

(choh-shee)
Chōshi ga, yoku arimasen.
condition
It doesn't run well.

_____

(neh-jee)(mah-keh-mah-sehn)
Neji o makemasen.
screw
I can't wind it.

_____

(gah-rah-soo-boo-tah) (tskeh-teh)
Garasubuta o   tsukete kudasai.
attach
I need a crystal.

_____

(deh-kee-mahs)
Itsu dekimasu ka.
When will it be ready?

_____

(reh-shee-toh)
Reshīto o onegai shimasu.
Can you give me a receipt?

_____

Try reading this paragraph to see if you can understand it. You may need to refer to the previous sentences.

(ah-roo hee)

Watakushi no tokei no chōshi ga, yoku arimasen. Aru hi wa susumigachi de,
one   day

(hoh-kah noh hee)   *(moht-teh eet-teh)*

hoka no hi wa okuregachi desu. Kyō wa, neji o makemasen. Tokeiya e motte itte, naoshite
another day   bring

(beh-kee-dehs)

morau bekidesu ka. Soretomo, tabun atarashii tokei o kau bekidesu.
should

1. If you are always arriving late, what could be wrong with your watch?

_____

2. When you always seem to be early for appointments, what might be the problem?

_____

23

(gee-foo-toh shohp-poo)
Gifuto shoppu
The Gift Shop

(reh-kōh-doh yah)　　*(oh-dee-oh sehn-mohn tehn)*
Rekōdo ya / Ōdio senmon ten
Record Store / Audio Equipment Store

(kah-meh-rah yah)
Kamera ya
Photography Shop

GIFUTO SHOPPU DE

okurimono
gift

(hahn-gah)
hanga
woodblock print

(tōh-kee)
tōki
pottery

(tah-keh kah-goh)
take kago
bamboo basket

(neen-gyōh)
ningyō
doll

shinju
pearls

(sheek-kee)
shikki
lacquerware

(kēē reen-goo)
kī ringu
key ring

(kah-meh-rah)
kamera
camera

(kah-mee-zah-ee-koo)
kamizaiku
papercraft

sukāfu
scarf

(byoh-boo)
byōbu
folding screen

(tah-koh)　　*(sehn-soo)*
tako　　**sensu**
kite　　fan

Mary Smith goes into a gift shop.

CLERK   **Irasshaimase.**   Can I help you?

                        (tehn-keh-teh-kee nah)
MARY   **Nanika tenkeiteki   na**   I would like something typically Japanese.

Nihon no mono ga hoshii no

desu ga.

CLERK   **Okurimono desu ka.**   For a gift?

                        (moht-teh kah-eh-roo)
MARY   **Hai. Kuni e motte   kaeru**   Yes. I need several gifts to take back home.

tame ni, okurimono ga irimasu.

            (oo-roo-shee) (oo-tsoo-wah)
CLERK   **Urushi no utsuwa wa**   How about a lacquer bowl? Or this handpainted

ikaga desu ka. Soretomo,   vase?

            (teh-noo-ree noh) (kah-been)
kono tenuri   no kabin wa.

MARY   **Hai. Kirei desu ne.**   Yes. They're lovely. I'll take them.

Sore o itadakimasu.

            (toh-koh-roh-deh)
CLERK   **Tokorode gojibun no**   How about a beautiful kimono for yourself?
            by the way
tame ni, utsukushii kimono wa

ikaga desu ka.

                        (deh-shoh)
MARY   **Totemo takai no desho.**   They must be very expensive.

CLERK   **Furui kinu no kimono wa**   The antique silk ones are reasonably priced.
(teh-goh-roh nah)   (oh-neh-dahn)
tegoro   na   onedan desu yo.

MARY   **Kono akai no wa**   This red one is gorgeous. I must have it!
                    (wah)   (zeht-tah-ee)
subarashii wa.   Zettai
                            absolutely
irimasu.

185

True or false? Choose the correct answer based on the dialogue.

1. Meri san wa, kuni e motte kaeru tame ni okurimono ga irimasu.   1. _____

2. Urushi no utsuwa o itadakimasu.   2. _____

3. Tenuri no kabin wa itadakimasen.   3. _____

4. Furui kinu no kimono wa tegoro na onedan desu.   4. _____

5. Merī san wa, akai kimono wa irimasen.   5. _____

REKŌDO YA DE
At the Record Store

(kah-seht-toh teͤh-poo)
kasetto tēpu
cassette tape

(kohn-pahk-toh dees-koo)
konpakuto disuku
CD (compact disc)

(reh-koͤh-doh)
rekōdo
record

(bee-deh-oh kah-seht-toh)
bideo kasetto
videocassette

(bee-deh-oh dees-koo)
bideo disuku
video disc

(koo-rah-sheek-koo)
kurashikku ongaku
classical music

(poh-pyoo-raͤh ohn-gah-koo)
popyurā   ongaku
pop music

ŌDIO SENMON TEN DE
At the Audio Equipment Store

rajio
radio

(teh-reh-bee)
terebi
television

(bee-deh-oh teͤh-poo reh-koͤh-daͤh)
bideo tēpu rekōdā
VCR

ANSWERS

True or False   1. True   2. True   3. False   4. True   5. False

(teh-poo reh-koh-dah)
tēpu rekōdā
tape recorder

(spee-kah)
supīkā
speakers

(rah-jee-kah-seh)
rajikase
radio cassette player

(kohn-pahk-toh dees-koo poo-reh-yah)
konpakuto disuku purēyā
CD player

Let's read a paragraph about listening to music.

Māku san to musuko no Pōru wa,
(koh-noh-mee)
ongaku no konomi ga totemo
taste
chigaimasu. Futari wa, rekōdo ya

e ikimasu. Māku san wa,

kurashikku ongaku ga suki desu.

Kare wa konpakuto disuku o
(kee-meh-rah-reh-mah-sehn)
mimasu ga, kimeraremasen.

(rohk-koo stah)
Pōru wa Nihon no rokku sutā no
(mee-tskeh-mahs)
kasetto o mitsukemasu. Kare wa

Amerika e motte kaeru tame ni
(ee-koots-kah)
sore o ikutsuka kaimasu.

Mark and his son, Paul, have very different taste in music. They go to a record store. Mark likes classical music. He looks at some CDs, but he can't make up his mind.

Paul finds some cassettes of Japanese rock stars. He buys several to take back to the States with him.

Can you unscramble these sentences?

1. ongaku / suki desu / Māku / ga / kurashikku / wa / san

_____

2. Nihon / mitsukemasu / kasetto / wa / Pōru / sutā / no / rokku / no / o

_____

187

KAMERA YA DE

At the Photography Shop

(shah-sheen)
shashin
print

(hee-kee-noh-bah-shee)
hikinobashi
enlargement

batterī
battery

(shah-sheen)
shashin ya
photography shop

(soo-rah-ee-doh)
suraido
slides

kamera
camera

(foo-ee-roo-moo)
fuirumu
roll of film

(bee-deh-oh kah-meh-rah)
bideo kamera
video camera

Here's a short dialogue that might take place in a photography shop. Try to read it aloud.

MARK **Watakushi no shashin wa dekite imasu ka.**

Are my prints ready?

CLERK **Hai. Koko ni arimasu.**

Yes. Here they are.

MARK **Tokorode, kono fuirumu o genzō shite kudasai. Kondo wa, suraido desu.**

Now I'd like this roll developed. This time I want slides.

188

CLERK	**Kashikomarimashita.**	Certainly, sir.
MARK	**Sorekara, 24 mai dori no 35 miri no karā fuirumu o ni hon kudasai.**	And I'd like two rolls of 35 millimeter color film with 24 exposures.
CLERK	**Hai, dōzo.**	Here you are, sir.

Be sure you thoroughly understand the dialogue before going on to the completion exercise below (and check your answers!).

1. Watakushi no s _____ w _____ dekite imasu ka.

2. Hai. K _____ n _____ a _____ .

3. T_____ , k _____ f _____ o genzō shite kudasai.

4. Kondo wa, s _____ desu.

5. K _____ .

(shōo-ree)
Shūri no sābisu
Repair Services

(koo-tsoo-nah-oh-shee)
Kutsunaoshi
The Shoemaker

(meh-gah-neh yah)
Megane ya
The Optician

KUTSUNAOSHI DE
At the Shoemaker

(koo-tsoo)
kutsu
shoes

(koo-tsoo hee-moh)
kutsu himo
shoelaces

(sahn-dah-roo)
sandaru
sandals

kutsunaoshi
shoemaker

Kono chikaku ni, kutsunaoshi ga *(aht-tah-rah)* **attara oshiete kudasai.**	Can you tell me if there is a shoemaker near here?
(kah-kah-toh) *(oh-reh-teh)* **Kakato ga orete shimaimashita.**	My heel is broken.
Matte iru aida ni, naoshite moraemasu ka.	Can you fix my shoe while I wait?
Itsu modotte kuru beki desu ka.	When should I come back?

(oh-boh-eh-teh)
Oboete kudasai
Remember

(ah-ee-teh) **aite iru**	to be open
(mah-deh) **made**	until
(soh-koh-gah-wah) **sokogawa**	sole

(soo-ree-kee-ree-tah)	
surikireta	worn
(soh-koh-gah-wah oh hah-reh-kah-eh-roo)	
sokogawa o harikaeru	to resole
(bee-nēē-roo)	
binīru	plastic
kawa	leather
(kah-ree noh)	
kari no	temporary
kakato	heel

MEGANE YA DE
At the Optician

megane ya
optician

(kohn-tahk-toh rehn-zoo)
kontakuto renzu
contact lens

(koh-wah-reh-tah)(meh-gah-neh)
kowareta megane
broken glasses

(foo-chee)
fuchi
frame

Read the following dialogue about the optician.

MARK	**Megane no fuchi to renzu**	The frame and a lens of my glasses are broken.
	ga kowarete shimaimashita.	Can you fix them?
	Naoshite moraemasu ka.	
OPTICIAN	*(yoh-bee noh)* **Yobi no megane o**	Do you have a spare pair?
	motte imasu ka.	
MARK	*(moht-teh ee-mah-sehn)* **Iie, motte imasen.**	No, I don't. And I can't see without them.
	(nah-shee nee-wah) **Soshite megane nashi niwa,**	
	watakushi wa miru koto ga	
	dekimasen.	
OPTICIAN	*(soh-reh-deh-wah) (ee-soh-ee-deh)* **Soredewa, isoide**	In that case, I'll fix them quickly. Come back
	(nah-oh-shee-mah-shōh) **naoshimashō. Ashita no asa**	tomorrow at 10 AM. They'll be ready.

(moh-doht-teh kee-teh)
jū ji ni, modotte kite

kudasai. Dekite imasu yo.

(tahs-kah-ree-mahs)
MARK   **Hontō ni, tasukarimasu.**   I'm very grateful.

Oboete kudasai
Remember

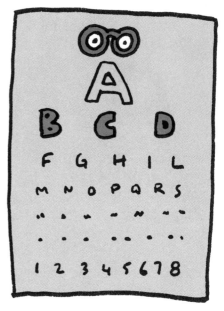

(nah-oh-soo)
naosu   to fix

(shee-meh-roo)
shimeru   to tighten

(sahn-goo-rah-soo)
sangurasu   sunglasses

(toh-ree-kah-eh-roo)
torikaeru   to replace

(soo-goo nee)
sugu ni   right away

(hee-bee gah hah-eet-teh)
hibi ga haitte   cracked

yobi no megane   a spare pair

After studying the shoemaker and optician vocabulary, try to match the Japanese words and their English equivalents.

1. sokogawa   a. heel
2. hibi ga haitte   b. temporary
3. naosu   c. sole
4. kawa   d. to replace
5. sokogawa o harikaeru   e. cracked
6. yobi no megane   f. right away
7. kakato   g. a spare pair
8. sugu ni   h. to fix
9. torikaeru   i. to resole
10. kari no   j. leather

ANSWERS

Matching 1. c 2. e 3. h 4. j 5. i 6. g 7. a 8. f 9. d 10. b

(sah-tsoo)
SATSU TO KŌKA
Bills and Coins

The basic unit of Japanese currency is the yen. The Japanese word for yen is **en**. The bills come in the following denominations:

1,000 **en**, 5,000 **en**, 10,000 **en**

Unlike U.S. dollars, each of the three **en** bills is a different size. The largest one, in both size and amount, is the 10,000 **en** bill.

The six coins are as follows:

500 **en**	silver color
100 **en**	silver color
50 **en**	silver color
10 **en**	bronze color
5 **en**	copper color
1 **en**	aluminum

You can exchange your currency for **en** at your hotel or at a bank. Japanese banks are open Monday through Friday from 9 A.M. to 3 P.M.

GINKŌ, GAIKA KŌKAN, TO TORABERĀ CHEKKU

(gah-ee-kah koh-kahn) *(toh-rah-beh-rah chehk-koo)*

Banks, Money Exchange, and Traveler's Checks

Hito to Mono

People and Things

(geen-koh-een)
ginkōin
bank employee

ginkō
bank

(gehn-keen)
genkin
cash

(kah-shee-tskeh keen)
kashitsuke kin
loan (money you borrow)

(mah-doh-goo-chee-gah-kah-ree)
madoguchigakari
teller

okane
money

(geen-koh teh-gah-tah)
ginkō tegata
banknote

(mah-doh-goo-chee)
madoguchi
teller's window

(yoh-keen hyoh)
yokin hyō
deposit slip

(koh-zah)
kōza
account

(mah-neh-jah)
manējā
manager

(koh-geet-teh-choh)
kogittechō
checkbook

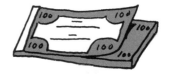

toraberā chekku
traveler's check

(koh-mah-kah-ee oh-kah-neh)
komakai okane
small change

194

Mark Smith enters a Tokyo bank. After standing in line, he approaches the teller.

MARK **Konnichiwa. Kono 100** *(hyah-koo)*
doru no Amerika no toraberā *(doh-roo)*
chekku o, en ni kaete kudasai. *(kah-eh-teh)*

Good day, sir. I need to exchange this $100 American traveler's check for Japanese yen.

TELLER **Wakarimashita. Chekku** *(chehk-koo)*
ni sainshite kudasai. *(sah-een-shteh)*

Sorekara, pasupōto o misete

itadakemasu ka.

Very well. Please sign the check. And may I have your passport, please?

MARK **Hai, dōzo.**

Here it is.

TELLER **En wa ōkii osatsu ga** *(oh-sah-tsoo)*

ii desu ka, soretomo chiisai

no ga ii desu ka.

Would you like the yen in large bills or small ones?

MARK **Chiisai osatsu o onegai**

shimasu.

Small bills, please.

TELLER **Wakarimashita. Sumisu**

san, asoko ni okake kudasai.
Dekitara onamae o *(deh-kee-tah-rah)*
oyobishimasu. *(oh-yoh-bee-shee-mahs)*

Please have a seat over there, Mr. Smith. I'll call your name when it's ready.

(After five minutes, Mark hears his name called and goes back to the teller.)

TELLER **Sumisu san, dōzo.**   Here's your money, Mr. Smith.

MARK   **Arigatō gozaimashita.**   Thank you. Goodbye.

       Sayōnara.

SHIKATA
How to

(kōh-kahn-soo-roo)
kōkansuru
to exchange

(kōh-kahn ree-tsoo)
kōkan ritsu
rate of exchange

(hah-rah-oo)
harau
to pay

(kōh-zah oh hee-rah-koo)
kōza o hiraku
to open an account

(yoh-keen)   *(yoh-keen-soo-roo)*
yokin   **yokinsuru**
deposit   to deposit

(hee-kee-dahs)
hikidasu
to withdraw

(sah-een-soo-roo)
sainsuru
to sign

(koh-geet-teh) (gehn-keen-kah-soo-roo)
kogitte o   genkinkasuru
to cash a check

196

Now see if you can remember these useful things. Match each expression or word to each picture by checking off the appropriate box.

1. madoguchigakari ☐
   yokin hyō ☐

2. komakai okane ☐
   kogittechō ☐

3. yokinsuru ☐
   sainsuru ☐

4. ginkō tegata ☐
   ginkō ☐

5. kōkansuru ☐
   toraberā chekku ☐

6. kōkan ritsu ☐
   genkin ☐

Now have fun with this crossword puzzle about money and banking.

ACROSS

1. exchange rate
3. money
5. dollars
7. manager
9. small bills
11. teller's window
13. bank

DOWN

2. deposit
3. large bills
4. yen
6. traveler's check
8. cash
10. to sign
12. account

26 *(yōo-been kyoh-koo) (noh) (sāh-bee-soo)*
Yūbin kyoku no sābisu
Postal Service

Post offices are identified by this symbol: 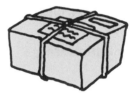 It looks like a capital **T** with a bar above it. Mailboxes on the street have this symbol too.

The easiest way to send your mail is to ask your hotel front desk staff to help you. They will either mail things for you, or they will direct you to the nearest mailbox or the appropriate post office.

(yōo-been-yah sahn)
yūbinya san
mailman

(koh-zoo-tsoo-mee)
kozutsumi
package

(yōo-been) (teh-gah-mee) *(hah-gah-kee)*
yūbin / tegami / hagaki
mail / letters / cards

(yōo-been kyoh-koo)
yūbin kyoku
post office

(keet-teh)
kitte
stamps

(dehn-pōh)
denpō
telegram

(pohs-toh)
posuto
mailbox

(mah-doh-goo-chee)/(yōo-been kyoh-koo-een)
madoguchi / yūbin kyokuin
window / post office employee

Mark wants to mail a package to the United States. Anne goes with him to the post office.

MARK **Dono madoguchi ga hitsuyō**
(deh-shōh kah)
deshō ka.

I wonder which window we need.

ANNE
(tah-meh-shteh) (mee-mah-shōh)
Kore o, tameshite mimashō.

Let's try this one.

MARK **Sumimasen ga. Kono**

kozutsumi o Amerika e
(oh-koo-ree-tah-ee)
okuritai no desu ga.

Excuse me. I want to mail this package to the United States.

CLERK **Mochiron desu. Saisho**
(zēh-kahn) (yōh-shee)
ni, kono zēkan no yōshi ni
(kah-kee-kohn-deh) (kōh-kōo-been)
kakikonde kudasai. Kōkūbin

de okuritai desu ka, soretomo
(foo-nah-been)
funabin de okuritai desu ka.

Of course. Just fill out this customs forms first.

Do you want to send it air mail or sea mail?

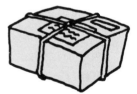

MARK **Kōkūbin o onegai shimasu.**

Air mail, please.

CLERK
(yōo-been ryōh-keen)
Sō desu nē, yūbin ryōkin
(nee nah-ree-mahs)
wa 3500 en ni narimasu.
comes to

Let's see . . . the postage comes to 3,500 yen.

MARK
(choht-toh) (kahn-gah-eh)
Chotto, kangae o
(kah-eh-mahsh-tah)
kaemashita. Funabin de ii

desu.

I just changed my mind. Sea mail will be fine!

200

ANNE **Kitte o katte, sorekara** *(keet-teh) (kaht-teh)*

tegami o dashitai desu. *(dahsh-tah-ee)*

I want to buy some stamps and mail some letters.

CLERK **Tegami o kuretara,** *(koo-reh-tah-rah)*

mekata o hakarimasu. *(meh-kah-tah oh hah-kah-ree-mahs)*

If you give me the letters, I'll weigh them.

ANNE **Hai, dōzo.**

Here they are.

CLERK **200 en itadakimasu.** *(nee hyah-koo)(ee-tah-dah-kee-mahs)*

That will be 200 yen.

ANNE **Onaji madoguchi de subete**

kaeru. Nante benri nandeshō. *(kah-eh-roo) (Nahn-teh) (behn-ree) (nahn-deh-shoh)*

Everything at the same window. How convenient!

True or false? After you have read the dialogue several times, read these sentences and choose the correct answer.

1. Māku san wa, kono kozutsumi o Furansu e okuritai desu.

1. _____

2. Kōkūbin de kozutsumi o okuru no wa, totemo takai desu.

2. _____

3. Kare wa, sore o funabin de okurimasu.

3. _____

4. An san wa, hagaki o sukoshi kaitai desu.

4. _____

5. Kyokuin wa, tegami no mekata o hakarimasu.

5. _____

6. Yūbin ryōkin wa, 300 en desu.

6. _____

201

Dōshi o mō sukoshi

More verbs

Here are some useful verbs. Notice that in Japanese two different verbs are used for sending letters and packages.

(dahs)
Dasu is used for sending letters (it has many other meanings as well, but for now, just learn
(oh-koo-roo)
this one). **Okuru** means mail, not send, and it's used for packages, gifts, and other items.

	(dahs) **dasu** to send [a letter]	
	AFFIRMATIVE	NEGATIVE
PRESENT	*(dah-shee-mahs)* **dashimasu**	*(dah-shee-mah-sehn)* **dashimasen**
PAST	*(dah-shee-mahsh-tah)* **dashimashita**	**dashimasen deshita**

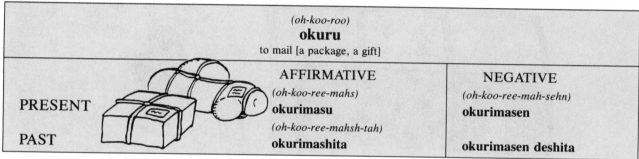

	(oh-koo-roo) **okuru** to mail [a package, a gift]	
	AFFIRMATIVE	NEGATIVE
PRESENT	*(oh-koo-ree-mahs)* **okurimasu**	*(oh-koo-ree-mah-sehn)* **okurimasen**
PAST	*(oh-koo-ree-mahsh-tah)* **okurimashita**	**okurimasen deshita**

Bunpō o mō sukoshi

More Grammar

Connecting Two Clauses

It's useful to know how to connect two independent clauses into one sentence. You can do this by changing the verb in the first clause to the **-te** form. Here's how it looks:

Mark goes to the post office, and he mails a package. **Māku san wa, yūbin kyoku e itte, kozutsumi o okurimasu.**

That's easy, isn't it? Now try a few yourself.

Fill in the correct form of the verb in the following sentences.

1. Tarō san wa, mainichi panya e _____ , pan o kaimasu.
   goes

2. Merī san wa, mai asa tōsuto o _____ , miruku o nomimasu.
   eats

ANSWERS

Sentences 1. itte 2. tabete

202

3. Shinbun o _____ , watakushi ni kudasai.
   buy

4. Tegami o _____ , hoteru e modorimasu.
   mail

5. Basu ni _____ , Ginza de orimasu.
   get on

Let's end with an easy one: Fill in the Japanese expression for each picture.

1. _____   2. _____   3. _____

4. _____   5. _____   6. _____

(moh-shee moh-shee)
MOSHI MOSHI
Hello? Hello?

Moshi moshi. — Hello?

(doh-nah-tah)
Donata desu ka. — Who is it?

Watakushi wa, — This is . . .

. . . desu.

(hah-nahsh-tah-ee)
. . . to, hanashitai no — I would like to speak to . . .

desu ga.

(dehn-gohn) *(noh-koh-shteh-moh)*
Dengon o nokoshitemo ii — May I leave a message?

desu ka.

. . . ni, Māku Sumisu — Tell . . . that Mark Smith will call back later.
(ah-toh deh)
ga ato de mata denwa
(ohts-tah-eh)
suru to otsutae kudasai.

(kōh-kahn-shoo)
Kokanshu san. — Operator! (speaking to the operator)

Setsuzoku ga, yoku arimasen. — This is a bad connection.

(kee-reh-teh)
Denwa ga, kirete shimaimashita. — We have been cut off.

(mah-chee-gah-ee dehn-wah)
Machigai denwa desu. — This is the wrong number.

(joo-sheen-neen bah-rah-ee noh dehn-wah)
Jushinnin barai no denwa o — I would like to make a collect call.
(kah-keh-tah-ee)
kaketai no desu ga.

(pah-soh-nah-roo koh-roo)
Pāsonaru kōru o kaketai no

desu ga.

I would like to make a person-to-person call.

(kee-rah-nah-ee-deh)
Kiranaide kudasai.

Don't hang up.

(choht-toh oh-mah-chee koo-dah-sah-ee)
Chotto, omachi kudasai.

Just a minute, please.

(dah-ee-yah-roo oh mah-wah-soo)
daiyaru o mawasu

to dial a number

(joo-wah-kee)(toh-ree-ah-geh-roo)
juwaki o toriageru

to pick up the receiver

(dehn-wah nee deh-roo)
denwa ni deru

to answer the phone

(dehn-wah oh kee-roo)
denwa o kiru

to hang up

(dehn-wah choh)
denwa chō

telephone book

(dehn-wah bohk-koo-soo)
denwa bokkusu

telephone booth

(koh-kahn-shoo) (oh-peh-reh-tah)
kōkanshu / operētā

operator

(dehn-wah bahn-goh)
denwa bangō

telephone number

(teh-reh-fohn-kah-doh)
terefonkādo

telephone card

The easiest way to make a telephone call is to do it from your hotel. There the hotel staff can help you if you need it.

For a **person-to-person international call,** ask for an English-speaking operator. For a **station-to-station call,** get the country and city code, and you can dial it yourself. When using **public phones,** keep in mind that a 3-minute local call costs 10 yen. You lift the receiver, deposit your coins, wait for a dial tone, then dial the number. If you're going to speak for more than 3 minutes, insert the coins at the beginning, or you may be cut off abruptly. If you do hear a warning tone, insert more coins immediately. Any unused coins will be returned at the end of your call. Most convenient? Use a telephone card, which you can buy at a nearby vending machine or kiosk.

KŌSHŪ DENWA

Public Pay Phones

telephone
card
machine

gray telephone

green telephone

red telephone

Most public phones are green or gray. Both take telephone cards; most take coins as well, although some green ones don't. Red phones take only 10-yen coins.

Here are some more useful expressions for using the telephone:

(choh-kyoh-ree dehn-wah)

Chōkyori denwa o kaketai no
                    I'd like to make a long-distance call.

desu ga.

Watakushi wa . . . ni denwa o
                    I'd like to make a call to . . .

kaketai no desu ga.

(kohk-sah-ee dehn-wah)   *(oh-peh-reh-tah)*

Kokusai denwa no operētā o
                    Please connect me with the international

onegai shimasu.
                    operator.

Eigo o hanasu operētā o onegai
                    I'd like an English-speaking operator, please.

shimasu.

(dehn-wah bahn-goh)

Sono denwa bangō wa shirimasen.
             I don't know the phone number.

(fahk-koo-soo)

fakkusu

fax

DENWA BOKKUSU DE

At the Telephone Booth

Mark and Mary are at a public phone booth in Tokyo. Mark is calling a Japanese friend, Mr. Yamada.

MARK **Sō desu nē, juwaki o**
(koh-kah) (ee-reh-teh) (tsoo-wah
totte, kōka o irete, tsūwa
ohn)
on o matte, sorekara daiyaru

o mawashimasu.

Let's see. I lift the receiver, put the coins in, wait for a dial tone, and dial the number.

RECEPTIONIST **Moshi moshi.**

Hello?

MARK **Moshi moshi. Yamada san**

o onegai shimasu.

Hello. May I speak to Mr. Yamada, please?

RECEPTIONIST **Shōshō omachi**
(shoh-shoh oh-mah-chee
koo-dah-sah-ee)
kudasai.

Just a minute please.

(Mr. Yamada finally comes on the line.)

MR. YAMADA **Moshi moshi.**

Hello?

MARK **Moshi moshi, Yamada san**

desu ka. Watakushi wa, Māku

Sumisu desu.

Hello, Mr. Yamada? This is Mark Smith.

MR. YAMADA **Sumisu san, ogenki**

desu ka.

Mr. Smith, how are you?

MARK	**Hai, okagesama de. Denwa** *(ree-yōō)* **shita riyū wa . . .**	I'm fine, thanks. The reason I'm calling is . . .

(Suddenly there's a loud BEEP on the line)

MARK	**Are wa, nan desu ka.**	What's that?
MR. YAMADA	*(ee-SOH-ee-deh)* **Isoide. 10 en kōka** *(ee-reh-teh)* **o mō sukoshi irete kudasai.**	Quick! Deposit some more 10-yen coins!
MARK	**Motte imasen. Merī, 10** *(skoh-shee)* **en kōka o sukoshi kudasai.** *(shee-MAHT-tah)* *(oh-soh-soo-gee-roo)* ***Shimatta.*** **Ososugiru. Denwa ga kirete shimaimashita.**	I don't have one! Mary, give me some 10-yen coins! Darn it—too late. I've been cut off.

* Men only—women don't use this expression.

After studying the expressions at the beginning of this section and the dialogue, can you fill in the blanks in these sentences?

1. _____ o nokoshitemo ii desu ka.
       message

2. _____ desu.
       wrong number

3. _____ o onegai shimasu.
       international operator

4. _____ kudasai.
       just a minute

5. Sono denwa bangō wa _____ .
       don't know

ANSWERS

Dialogue 1. Dengon 2. Machigai denwa 3. Kokusai denwa no operētā/kōkanshi 4. Shōshō omachi 5. shirimasen

208

Here's a word search puzzle for you to enjoy. Find the Japanese expressions for the words listed, and circle them.

telephone number, hello, receiver, coins, telephone book, telephone booth, long distance call, yen

J	D	K	B	Q	M	A	Z	O	T	N	A	S	I
D	E	N	W	A	B	O	K	K	U	S	U	E	P
E	N	A	E	C	Y	K	L	E	Q	U	D	K	J
S	W	R	B	N	A	P	Q	S	I	P	E	H	U
F	A	I	T	U	N	M	E	C	L	D	S	U	W
Q	C	H	O	K	Y	O	R	I	D	E	N	W	A
Y	H	A	Q	T	S	S	C	D	K	N	H	L	K
P	O	R	I	V	U	H	K	A	J	W	B	R	I
S	T	B	H	I	T	I	B	E	V	A	H	U	H
E	N	M	A	Y	F	M	A	Q	O	B	E	C	F
G	T	I	N	E	X	O	R	O	P	A	M	T	O
J	U	W	U	B	O	S	W	F	E	N	S	A	K
A	S	C	P	U	R	H	I	T	U	G	A	N	W
V	C	U	L	F	S	I	Z	A	K	O	K	A	D

(ah-tah-mah) *(tsoo-mah-sah-kee)*

ATAMA KARA TSUMASAKI MADE

From Head to Toe

Mark and Mary are testing each other on the parts of the body in Japanese. It's a good way to learn the counters, too!

MARK	**Dare ga, hajimemasu** *(hah-jee-meh-mahs)* **ka. Anata, soretomo watakushi.**	Who'll start, you or I?
MARY	**Saisho ni, anata ga watakushi ni kiite kudasai.**	You ask me first.

MARK	**Ii desu yo. Kore wa nan desu ka.**		Good. What is that?
MARY	*(kah-mee-noh-keh)* **Kaminoke.**		The hair.
MARK	**Me no aida ni aru no wa.**		And between the eyes?
MARY	*(hah-nah)* **Hana.**		The nose.
MARK	**Hana to kuchi no** *(koo-chee)* **aida ni atte, aru** *(ah-roo)*		Between the nose and the mouth, some men grow

otoko no hito ga
(hah-yah-soo)
hayasu mono wa

MARY   *(koo-chee hee-geh)*
MARY   **kuchi hige.**

a mustache.

MARK   *(mee-mee)*
MARK   **Mimi ga futatsu**

You have two ears

atte,

MARY   *(hoh-oh)*
MARY   **hoo ga futatsu,**

and two cheeks,

MARK   *(kah-oh)*
MARK   **keredomo kao wa**

but only one face

hitotsu dake de,

MARY   **atama mo hitotsu**

and only one head.

dake desu.

MARK   *(wah-rah-oo)* *(mee-eh-roo)*
MARK   **Warau to mieru**
             visible

When you laugh, one sees

no ga,

MARY   *(hah)*
MARY   **ha**

the teeth

MARK   **soshite isha**

and when you go to the doctor, you show him

ni ikuto, miseru

no ga,

MARY   *(shtah)*
MARY   **shita.**

your tongue.

MARK   **Kore wa**

This is

MARY   *(ah-goh)*
MARY   **ago**

the chin

MARK   **soshite sore wa**

and that is

MARY   *(koo-bee)*
MARY   **kubi desu.**

the neck.

MARK   **Koko no futatsu**

Here are two

wa

MARY **kata** *(kah-tah)*

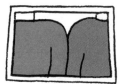

shoulders

MARK **soshite futatsu no**

and two

MARY **hiji** *(hee-jee)*

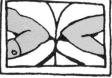

elbows—

MARK **futatsu no**

two

MARY **te** *(teh)*

hands

MARK **soshite juppon no**

and ten

MARY **yubi** *(yoo-bee)*

fingers.

MARK **Kondo wa,** *(kohn-doh)*
watakushi no ban *(bahn)*
desu.

Now it's my turn.

MARY **Kore wa**

This is

MARK **senaka** *(seh-nah-kah)*

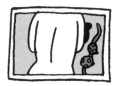

the back,

MARY **soshite mae ni aru no ga**

and here in front

MARK **mune desu.** *(moo-neh)*

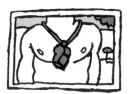

is the chest.

MARY **Soshite ushiro ni aru no ga**

And there in back is

MARK **oshiri.** *(oh-shee-ree)*

the fanny.

MARY **Soshite koko kara koko made**

And from here to here you have two

212

futatsu aru no ga

MARK   *(moh-moh)* **momo**   thighs

MARY   **kono futatsu ga**   and then two

MARK   *(hee-zah)* **hiza.**   knees.

MARY   **Soshite mō**   And farther down the two

sukoshi shita ni

futatsu aru no ga

MARK   *(foo-koo-rah-hah-gee)* **fukurahagi**   calves,

MARY   *(ah-shee-koo-bee)* **ashikubi made ga**   to the two ankles, are

MARK   *(ah-shee)* **ashi**   the feet

MARY   **juppon aru no ga**   with the ten

MARK   *(ah-shee-yoo-bee)* **ashiyubi desu.**   toes.

Now draw lines between the matching words.

1. atama	a. tongue
2. hiza	b. shoulders
3. kata	c. ankles
4. kubi	d. eyes
5. ashikubi	e. back
6. mune	f. chest
7. shita	g. knees
8. senaka	h. neck
9. me	i. hands
10. te	j. head

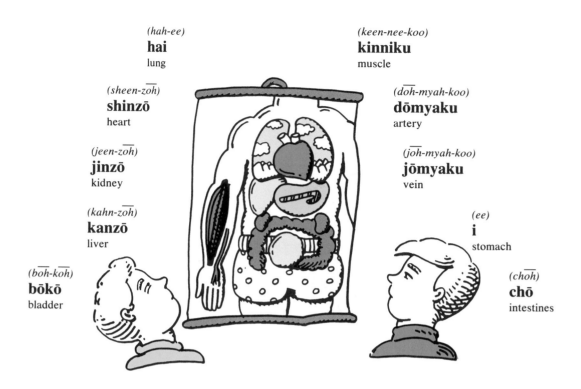

(hah-ee)
hai
lung

(keen-nee-koo)
kinniku
muscle

(sheen-zoh)
shinzō
heart

(doh-myah-koo)
dōmyaku
artery

(jeen-zoh)
jinzō
kidney

(joh-myah-koo)
jōmyaku
vein

(kahn-zoh)
kanzō
liver

(ee)
i
stomach

(boh-koh)
bōkō
bladder

(choh)
chō
intestines

(oh-boh-eh-teh)
Oboete imasu ka
Remember

In Chapter 18 you learned some of expressions for physical symptoms. The following list includes those and a few more. If you do become ill, the list will come in handy.

(oh-nah-kah) *(ee-tah-ee)*
Onaka ga itai desu.

(noh-doh)
Nodo ga itai desu.

Atama ga itai desu.

Ha ga itai desu.

(seh-kee) *(deh-mahs)*
Seki ga demasu.

(neh-tsoo)
Netsu ga arimasu.

(hah-kee-keh)
Hakike ga shimasu.

(hah-nah-jee)
Hanaji ga dete imasu.
nosebleed

My stomach hurts.

I have a sore throat.

I have a headache.

I have a toothache.

I have a cough.

I have a fever.

I feel like vomiting.

My nose is bleeding.

If you need to see a doctor or dentist while in Japan, your hotel staff can probably recommend one who speaks English. Still, it's a good idea to learn some of the expressions in these dialogues.

"Ā" TO ITTE KUDASAI
(ah)

Say "Aaah," Please.

Mary has a sore throat. She has an appointment with Dr. Morita, a general practitioner.

DR. MORITA **Sumisu san desu ka.**
(moh-ree-tah)
Watakushi ga Morita desu.

Doko ga warui desu ka.

Mrs. Smith? I'm Dr. Morita. What seems to be the matter?

MARY **Nodo ga, totemo itai desu.**

My throat is very sore.

(ah-keh-teh)
DR. MORITA **Kuchi o akete**

kudasai. "Ā" to itte kudasai.
(eh-eh)
Ee, nodo ga totemo akai desu
(shoh-jōh)
ne. Hoka niwa, nanika shōjō

ga arimasu ka.

Open your mouth, please. Say "Aah."

Yes, your throat is quite red. Are there any other symptoms?

(ee-tahk-teh)
MARY **Atama ga itakute,**
(tsoo-kah-reh-teh)
totemo tsukarete imasu.

My head aches and I'm very tired.

DR. MORITA **Netsu wa.**

Any fever?

MARY **Arimasu.**

Yes.

DR. MORITA **Kore ga**
(shoh-hoh-sehn)
shohōsen desu.
(koo-soo-ree) *(ee-chee-nee-chee)*
Kusuri o, ichinichi
(kah-ee)
san kai nonde kudasai.
(yoh-koo
Ni, san nichi de yoku
nah-rah-nah-keh-reh-bah)
naranakereba, denwa

shite kudasai.

Here's a prescription. Take the medicine three times a day. If you don't feel better in two or three days, please call me.

MARY **Arigatō gozaimashita.**

Thank you.

(oh-kee-koo)
ŌKIKU AKETE KUDASAI
Open wide!

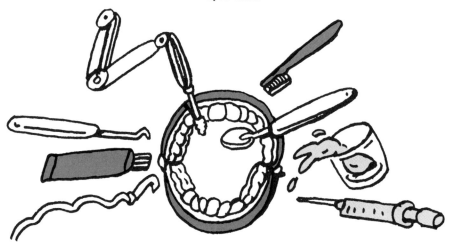

Mark has a toothache. A friend recommends a dentist, and Mark has a 2 o'clock appointment.

MARK **Watakushi wa Māku Sumisu**
(oh-shee-mah) *(sehn-seh)*
desu. Ni ji ni Ōshima   sensei
(mehn-kah-ee noh yahk-soh-koo)
to menkai   no yakusoku ga

arimasu.

I'm Mark Smith. I have an appointment with Dr. Oshima.

RECEPTIONIST **Wakarimashita.**

Dōzo okake kudasai.

Yes. Please take a seat.

216

(Mark waits for a few minutes.)

DENTAL ASSISTANT **Sumisu san.**
(koh-chee-rah eh)
Kochira   e. Kono isu ni

kakete kudasai. Sensei wa,
(moh-jee-kee)
mōjiki kimasu.

Mr. Smith? This way. Please sit in this chair. The doctor will be here soon.

DR. OSHIMA   **Sumisu san. Doko**
(shmeh-shteh)
ga itai ka shimeshite kudasai.

Mr. Smith? Can you show me where it hurts?

MARK   **Kono ha desu. Totemo**

itai desu.

It's this tooth. It's very sore.

(nah-roo-hoh-doh)
DR. OSHIMA   **Naruhodo.**

Wakarimashita.
(moo-shee-bah)
Mushiba desu.
(yoh-keh-reh-bah) (kah-ree
Yokereba,   kari
noh   tsoo-meh-moh-noh)
no tsumemono o shite,
(kah-eht-tah-rah)
kuni ni kaettara, anata
(hah-ee-shah)
no haisha ni mite moraemasu.

Yes. I can see. You have a cavity. If you like, I can give you a temporary filling now, and you can see your dentist when you get back home.

MARK   **Sore wa ii desu ne. Dōzo**

shite kudasai.

That's good. Go ahead.

(kyoh-koo-boo mah-soo-ee)
DR. OSHIMA   **Kyokubu   masui no**
(choo-shah)
chūsha o shimasu ka.

Would you like a shot of local anesthesia?

(shtah-koo   ah-ree-mah-sehn)
MARK   **Shitaku   arimasen. Demo**

shite kudasai.

No. But do it anyway.

Can you match up the words in the left column with the definitions in the right column?

1. shōjō
2. netsu
3. shohōsen
4. menkai no yakusoku
5. mushiba
6. kyokubu masui
7. kusuri
8. kari no tsumemono

a. fever
b. cavity
c. symptoms
d. medicine
e. local anesthesia
f. prescription
g. temporary filling
h. appointment

(byoh-een)
BYŌIN DE
At the Hospital

Joe Smith, Mark's uncle, has joined the Smith family in Tokyo. One evening, after dinner, he has symptoms which look like a heart attack. Mark rushes him to the hospital in an ambulance. Mary joins Mark in the waiting area.

(ee-teh-koo-reh-teh)

MARK **Merī, koko ni itekurete**
(tahs-kah-ree-mahs)
tasukarimasu. Watakushi wa,
(hohn-tōh nee) *(sheen-pah-ee shteh)*
hontō ni shinpai shite imasu.

I'm glad you're here, Mary. I'm really worried.

MARY **Ojisan wa, ima doko ni**

imasu ka.

Where is he now?

MARK *(kyoo-kahn noh chee-ryoh-shee-tsoo)*
Kyūkan no chiryōshitsu

ni imasu.

In the emergency room.

MARY *(kahn-goh-foo)*
Kangofu ga kimashita.

Here's the nurse.

MARK *(goo-ah-ee)*
Oji no guai wa, dō desu ka.
condition

How is my uncle?

NURSE *(dah-ee-joh-boo)*
Subete daijōbu desu.
(keh-tsoo-ah-tsoo) *(hah-kaht-teh)*
Sensei ga ketsuatsu o hakatte

imasu. Watakushi ni
(tsoo-ee-teh-kee-teh)
tsuitekite kudasai.

Everything is fine. The doctor is taking his blood pressure. Follow me.

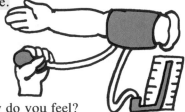

MARK **Sorede ojisan, guai wa dō**

desu ka.

So, Uncle Joe, how do you feel?

JOE *(nah-ree-mahsh-tah)*
Mae yori yoku narimashita.
became

Better than before.

MARK **Sensei, oji wa doko ga**

warui desu ka.

Doctor, what's the matter with my uncle?

DOCTOR **Kare wa, daijōbu desu.**

(tah-beh-soo-gee)
Bangohan no tabesugi ga
overeating
(gehn-een)
genin desu yo. Tokidoki
cause
(hee-doh-ee) *(shoh-kah foo-ryoh)* *(bah-ah-ee)*
hidoi shōka furyō no baai,

(sheen-zoh mah-hee) *(noh yoh nee mee-eh-roo)*
shinzō mahi no yō ni mieru

koto ga arimasu.

He'll be fine. It was that big dinner. Sometimes a bad case of indigestion can seem like a heart attack!

In Japanese, "doctor" is **isha**, and "dentist" is **haisha**. But when you speak *to* a doctor or dentist, or *about* one with office or hospital staff, use the polite term **sensei** instead. (Note: **sensei** is also used as a term of respect for a teacher.)

See if you can answer the following questions about the dialogues on the doctor, dentist, and hospital:

1. Merī san wa, naze isha ni ikimasu ka.
   (nah-zeh-nah-rah)
   A. Nazenara nodo ga itai kara desu.
   because
   B. Nazenara onaka ga itai kara desu.
   C. Nazenara seki ga deru kara desu.

2. Isha wa Meri san ni
   A. chūsha o shimasu.
   B. shohōsen o agemasu.
   C. kusuri o agemasu.

3. Māku san wa naze haisha ni ikimasu ka.
   A. Nazenara netsu ga aru kara desu.
   B. Nazenara hanaji ga dete iru kara desu.
   C. Nazenara ha ga itai kara desu.

4. Dare ga byōin e ikimasu ka.
   A. Pōru
   B. Tanaka san
   C. Jō ojisan

(keen-kyōo   jee-tah-ee) KINKYŪ JITAI

Emergencies

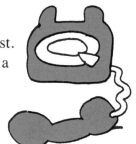

Japan is a safe country. Crime is rare and the people are generally honest. But on the off chance that you will have a medical or other emergency, it's a good idea to know some relevant words and phrases.

First, here are the vital phone numbers:

Police   110   Ambulance or Fire   119

You don't need a coin to dial these numbers from a public pay phone. Push the **red button** (there's one on every pay phone) first, then dial the three digits.

(kyōo-kyōo-shah) KYŪKYUSHA TO ISHA NO TASUKE *(tahs-keh)*

Ambulances and Medical Help

 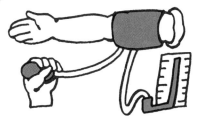

To get emergency medical help while in your hotel, ask the front desk staff. They can call an English-speaking doctor or send you to a hospital with English-speaking staff, such as St. Luke's International Hospital (**Seiroka Byoin**) in Tokyo.

Here are some useful words and phrases for a medical emergency:

kyūkyūsha	**kinkyū jitai**	**byōin**
ambulance	emergency	hospital

(tsoo-reh-teh eet-teh)
Isha ni tsurete   itte kudasai.   Take me to a doctor.

(yohn-deh)
Isha o yonde kudasai.   Get a doctor for me.

Kyūkyūsha ga hitsuyō desu.   I need an ambulance.

(yohn-deh)
Kyūkyūsha o yonde kudasai.   Call an ambulance.

221

Ashi no hone ga orete
(hoh-neh) *(oh-reh-teh)*

shimaimashita.

My leg is broken.

Shinzō mahi desu.
(sheen-zoh mah-hee)

I'm having a heart attack.

Dōki ga shimasu.
(doh-kee)

I'm having palpitations.

KEISATSU
(keh-sah-tsoo)
The Police

keikan / omawari san
(keh-kahn) (oh-mah-wah-ree sahn)
policeman

kōban
(koh-bahn)
police substation

Small police substations, called **kōban**, are located on many street corners in Japanese cities. If you have problems, the police can help you—from finding your way to finding lost items. In Japan, if you lose something, it may very well turn up. Even if you leave something in a taxi or on the subway, don't assume it's gone forever. As usual, you can ask your hotel front desk staff for help, or check with the police. In Tokyo, they can call the Central Lost and Found.

Here are some expressions you should know in case you need the police.

Moyori no keisatsu sho o
(moh-yoh-ree noh) (keh-sah-tsoo shoh)
police station

oshiete kudasai.

Please show me where the nearest police station is.

Tasukete kudasai. Keikan o

yonde kudasai.

Help! Call the police.

Pasupōtō o nakushite
(nah-koo-shteh)

shimaimashita.

I've lost my passport.

Saifu o nusumarete
(sah-ee-foo) (noo-soo-mah-reh-teh)

shimaimashita.

My wallet was stolen.

Michi ni mayotte shimaimashita.
(mah-yoht-teh)

I'm lost.

222

BEFORE YOU LEAVE

Shuppatsu no mae ni

You've learned a lot of Japanese by now—probably much more than you realize. This section is an important final step in the learning process—a step in which you review and solidify your understanding of your new language.

The section is organized around basic situations tourists may encounter. For each situation there are a number of questions about appropriate Japanese expressions. If you have difficulty remembering what to say in a particular situation, review the relevant chapter of this book.

Good luck!

Jōkyō 1: Hito to shiriau
Situation 1: Getting to Know People

1. It is afternoon and you meet someone. What do you say to start a conversation?
   A. Ohayō gozaimasu.
   B. Konnichiwa.
   C. Sayōnara.

2. You have just run into a friend whom you haven't seen in a while. What do you say?
   A. Dōmo arigatō.
   B. Sayōnara.
   C. Ogenki desu ka.

3. You want to get someone's attention. You say:
   A. Chotto, sumimasen ga.
   B. Hajimemashite.
   C. Iie, dō itashimashite.

4. It is evening. How do you greet someone?
   A. Konbanwa.
   B. Konnichiwa.
   C. Ohayō gozaimasu.

5. You have just been introduced to someone. You say:
   A. Hai.
   B. Hajimemashite.
   C. Arigatō gozaimasu.

Jōkyō 2: Tōchaku

Situation 2: Arrival

1. You have a reservation for two rooms at the hotel. What do you say?
   A. Erebētā wa, doko desu ka.
   B. Futa heya yoyaku ga shite arimasu.
   C. Nagame wa, ii desu ka.

2. The clerk asks how long you will be staying. You reply:
   A. Hai, dōzo.
   B. Watakushi no namae wa, Māku Sumisu desu.
   C. Yaku isshūkan tomarimasu.

3. You want to inquire whether breakfast is included in the price of the room. So you say:
   A. Shukuhaku dai ni chōshoku wa fukumarete imasu ka.
   B. Basurūmu ga arimasu ka.
   C. Mēdo ga imasu ka.

Jōkyō 3: Kankō kenbutsu

Situation 3: Seeing the Sights

1. You are on foot and you want to find a certain museum. You ask someone:
   A. Chotto sumimasen ga, bijutsukan niwa dō ittara ii ka oshiete kudasai.
   B. Chotto sumimasen ga, doko kara irrasshaimashita ka.
   C. Chotto sumimasen ga, yūbin kyoku niwa dō ittara ii ka oshiete kudasai.

2. The person might give you various directions, such as:
   A. Migi ni magatte kudasai.
   B. Kare ni agete kudasai.
   C. Koko ni kite kudasai.

3. You have just gotten onto a bus. You want to ask where to get off. You say:
   A. Doko de basu ni norimasu ka.
   B. Doko de basu o orimasu ka.
   C. Basu no tērūjo wa doko desu ka.

4. Someone on the street approaches you to ask you the time. He says:
   A. Chotto sumimasen ga, nanji desu ka.
   B. Chotto sumimasen ga, nan gatsu desu ka.
   C. Chotto sumimasen ga, nan nichi desu ka.

ANSWERS

Situation 2 1. B 2. C 3. A   Situation 3 1. A 2. A 3. B 4. A

224

5. You are at the train station and want to know the price of a round trip ticket to Kyoto. You ask:
   A. Kyoto yuki no ōfuku ken wa ikura desu ka.
   B. Watakushi wa Kyoto kara kimashita.
   C. Kyoto yuki no kisha wa, nanji ni demasu ka.

6. The clerk asks if you want regular or first class. He might say something like this:
   A. Gurīn sha ga ii desu ka, futsū ga ii desu ka.
   B. Shitei seki ni shimasu ka, jiyū seki ni shimasu ka.
   C. Kitsuen seki ga ii desu ka, kinen seki ga ii desu ka.

7. You want to say to someone that you are American and speak a little Japanese. You might say:
   A. Watakushi wa Amerikajin de eigo o hanashimasu.
   B. Watakushi wa Amerikajin de Nihongo o sukoshi hanashimasu.
   C. Watakushi wa Amerika kara kimashita.

8. You want to rent a car. You ask the clerk:
   A. Uchi o karitai no desu ga.
   B. Heya o karitai no desu ga.
   C. Kuruma o karitai no desu ga.

9. You want to fill up your car. You might say:
   A. Mantan ni shite kudasai.
   B. Oiru o chekku shite kudasai.
   C. Mizu o chekku shite kudasai.

10. You are asking a camping employee if there are essential services. You would *not* say . . .
    A. Shawā ga arimasu ka.
    B. Nomimizu ga arimasu ka.
    C. Bijutsukan ga arimasu ka.

11. As an answer to "Kyō wa nan gatsu, nan nichi desu ka."
    (What's today's date?), you would *not* hear . . .
    A. Ni gatsu jushichi nichi desu.
    B. San gatsu wa tenki ga ii desu.
    C. Ichigatsu tsuitachi desu.

12. To ask an airline employee what time your flight (flight 201) leaves, you would say:
    A. Sumimasen ga, ni hyaku ichi bin wa itsu demasu ka.
    B. Sumimasen ga, kisha wa itsu demasu ka.
    C. Sumimasen ga, kono bin dewa, shokuji ga demasu ka.

13. You want to make conversation about the weather. You would *not* say:
    A. Kyō wa donna tenki desu ka.
    B. Kyō wa kayōbi desu ka.
    C. Kyō wa samui desu ka.

Jōkyō 4: Goraku

Situation 4: Entertainment

1. You are discussing what to do that evening. You would *not* say:
   A. Kabuki gekijō wa dō desu ka.
   B. Eiga wa dō desu ka.
   C. Gakkō wa dō desu ka.

2. If someone were to ask you what your favorite sport was (Anata ga suki na supōtsu wa nan desu ka.), you would *not* say . . .
   A. Tenisu desu.
   B. Nihongo desu.
   C. Jogingu desu.

Jōkyō 5: Tabemono no chūmon

Situation 5: Ordering Food

1. You want to ask what the restaurants in Japan are like. You would ask . . .
   A. Nihon no resutoran wa dō desu ka.
   B. Nihon de resutoran wa doko ni arimasu ka.
   C. Nihon ni resutoran wa arimasu ka.

2. As a possible answer, you would *not* hear . . .
   A. Tokyo ni arimasu.
   B. Totemo subarashii desu.
   C. Totemo ii desu.

3. When a waiter asks if you want to order, he might say . . .
   A. Owarimashita ka.
   B. Kōhī wa ikaga desu ka.
   C. Gochūmon o ukagaimashō ka.

4. To see the menu, you would say . . .
   A. Mizu o onegai shimasu.
   B. Menyū o onegai shimasu.
   C. Chekku o onegai shimasu.

5. Which of the following is not connected with eating?
   A. restoran
   B. osara
   C. doraggusutoā

6. To order a certain vegetable you would say:
   A. Asuparagasu o kudasai.
   B. Sūpu o kudasai.
   C. Pan o kudasai.

7. If you choose **sūpu**, you need:
   A. fōku
   B. naifu
   C. supūn

8. An example of a dessert you might order is:
   A. aisukurīmu
   B. ika
   C. bishisoa

9. At the end of the meal, you say to the waiter/waitress:
   A. Sumimasen ga, ōdoburu o onegai shimasu.
   B. Sumimasen ga, shio to koshō o onegai shimasu.
   C. Sumimasen ga, okanjō o onegai shimasu.

10. How would you ask if the tip is included on your bill?
    A. Otearai wa doko desu ka.
    B. Sābisu ryō wa haitte imasu ka.
    C. Okanjō wa tadashii desu ka.

Jōkyō 6: Mise de
Situation 6: At the Store

1. Which of the following would you *not* say in a clothing store?
   A. Sūtsu ga irimasu.
   B. Pan o kaitai desu.
   C. Watakushi no Amerika no saizu wa 42 desu.

2. One of the following lists has nothing to do with clothing . . .
   A. yasai, niku, kudamono
   B. adai sukāto, kuroi handobaggu, kiiro no burausu
   C. shitagi, beruto, zubon

3. You would *not* hear which of the following in a butcher shop?
   A. Sono niku wa, oishisō desu.
   B. Hamu wa, ikura desu ka.
   C. Kudamono wa, ikura desu ka.

4. You want to get some medicine at a pharmacy. You might say:
   A. Kono kusuri o onegai shimasu.
   B. Kono tabemono o onegai shimasu.
   C. Kono yasai o onegai shimasu.

5. A pharmacist would *not* ask you one of the following:
   A. Osake ga irimasu ka.
   B. Taionkei ga irimasu ka.
   C. Asupirin ga irimasu ka.

ANSWERS

Situation 6   1. B 2. A 3. C 4. A 5. A   Situation 5   7. C 8. A 9. C 10. B

227

6. You are at the laundry. You would *not* say one of the following:
   A. Waishatsu niwa, nori o kakenaide kudasai.
   B. Kutsu o kaitai desu.
   C. Sentaku mono ga arimasu.

7. You are at the barber's and want a haircut. You might say:
   A. Sanpatsu shite kudasai.
   B. Ken o kudasai.
   C. Tabako o kudasai.

8. The hairdresser might ask you:
   A. Shinbun wa ikaga desu ka.
   B. Pēsutorī wa ikaga desu ka.
   C. Pāmanento wa ikaga desu ka.

Match up the following:

1. Utsukushi yubiwa ga irimasu.   A. Gifuto shoppu

2. Take no kago ga, kaitai desu.   B. Hōshokuten

3. Kono fuirumu o genzō shite kudasai.   C. Kamera ya

4. Konpakuto disuku purēyā o kaitai desu.   D. Shinbun uriba

5. Shinbun wa doko de kaimasu ka.   E. Tokei ya

6. Tokei ga susumigachi desu.   F. Ōdio senmon ten

7. Fūtō wa doko de kaimasu ka.   G. Megane ya

8. Megane ga kowarete shimaimashita.   H. Bunbōgu ten

Jōkyō 7: Taisetsu na sābisu
Situation 7: Essential Services

1. You are at a bank and wish to exchange a traveler's check . . .
   A. Kono toraberā chekku o kaete kudasai.
   B. En o kaitai no desu ga.
   C. Jikan o shiritai no desu ga.

2. A bank employee would *not* ask you . . .
   A. Chekku ni sainshite kudasai.
   B. En wa ōkii osatsu ga ii desu ka.
   C. Pan ga hoshii desu ka.

228

3. You want to buy stamps at a post office. You would say . . .
   A. Sumimasen ga, hagaki o kaitai desu.
   B. Sumimasen ga, kitte o kaitai desu.
   C. Sumimasen ga, chizu o kaitai desu.

4. Which of the following would you *not* say in a post office?
   A. Kono tegami o kōkūbin de dashitai no desu ga.
   B. Kono kozutsumi o funabin de okuritai no desu ga.
   C. Tomodachi ni denwa shitai desu.

5. You answer a phone call with . . .
   A. Sayonara.
   B. Moshi moshi.
   C. Dōmo arigatō.

6. You want to make a long distance phone call. You would say . . .
   A. Chōkyori denwa o kaketai no desu ga.
   B. Sono denwa bango wa shirimasen.
   C. Machigai denwa desu.

7. You would like an English-speaking operator. You would say . . .
   A. Dengon o nokoshitemo ii desu ka.
   B. Eigo o hanasu operētā o onegai shimasu.
   C. Setsuzoku ga, yoku arimasen.

8. You would *not* say one of the following to a doctor:
   A. Sensei, netsu ga arimasu.
   B. Sensei, kasa ga irimasu.
   C. Sensei, onaka ga itai desu.

9. The dentist asks you to show him where it hurts. You reply . . .
   A. Kono me desu.
   B. Kono yubi desu.
   C. Kono ha desu.

10. Which of the following would *not* be used to seek help in an emergency?
    A. Kyūkyūsha o yonde kudasai.
    B. Tasukete kudasai. Keikan o yonde kudasai.
    C. Niku ya e tsurete itte kudasai.

THE JAPANESE WRITING SYSTEM

Now that you have learned Japanese "the Fast and Fun Way," you may want to know something about the writing system. If so, these pages will help you get started.

Traditionally, Japanese is written from top to bottom and from right to left. But it is also written horizontally and from left to right, as in English.

Japanese writing uses three kinds of characters:

漢字 **kanji** (*kahn-jee*)

ひらがな **hiragana** (*hee-rah-gah-nah*)

カタカナ **katakana** (*kah-tah-kah-nah*)

Hiragana and katakana are also called **kana** (kah-nah). All three are used together in Japanese writing.

*Is the American Embassy nearby?

**Yes, it is. Go straight down this street, then turn left at the next intersection. It's right there.

KANJI

Chinese and Japanese are completely different languages. But beginning in the fourth or fifth century, Japanese adopted written symbols and many vocabulary items from Chinese. In Japan, these symbols or Chinese characters are called **kanji.** They represent both meaning and sound, and often one **kanji** has more than one pronunciation (or reading, as it's commonly called) and meaning.

Japanese people learn about 2,000 **kanji** by the end of high school. Those are the basic characters used in newspapers, magazines, and school textbooks. Most Japanese know several thousand additional **kanji** as well.

Kanji range from simple, with one or two strokes, to complex, with many strokes needed to make one character. Some look like pictures, or line drawings, of the words they represent.

mountain	**yama**	山	(*yah-mah*)
river	**kawa**	川	(*kah-wah*)

These two together form **Yamakawa,** 山川 a family name.

Here are some more **kanji:**

Japan	**Nihon** (*nee-hohn*)	日本
person	**hito** (*hee-toh*), **jin** (*jeen*)	人
Japanese	**Nihonjin** (*nee-hohn-jeen*)	日本人

HIRAGANA AND KATAKANA

Hiragana and **katakana** symbols represent the sounds of syllables. **Hiragana** is used for native Japanese words and grammatical elements, and **Katakana** is for words of foreign origin. Each is a kind of alphabet, or syllabary, of 46 basic characters or sounds.

The following example will show you how the elements are used together.

Welcome to Japan, Mr. Smith.
Sumisu san, Nihon e yōkoso.
スミスさん、日本へようこそ。

Smith	Mr.	Japan	to	welcome
Sumisu	**san**	**Nihon**	**e**	**yōkoso**
スミス	さん	日本	へ	ようこそ
katakana	hiragana	kanji		hiragana

The **hiragana** and **katakana** charts provided on the next two pages will help you to recognize some of the Japanese you'll see during your trip to Japan. And if you continue your study of Japanese in the future, you'll find them useful.

HIRAGANA

あ **a** (*ah*)	い **i** (*ee*)	う **u** (*oo*)	え **e** (*eh*)	お **o** (*oh*)
か **ka** (*kah*)	き **ki** (*kee*)	く **ku** (*koo*)	け **ke** (*keh*)	こ **ko** (*koh*)
さ **sa** (*sah*)	し **shi** (*shee*)	す **su** (*soo*)	せ **se** (*seh*)	そ **so** (*soh*)
た **ta** (*tah*)	ち **chi** (*chee*)	つ **tsu** (*tsoo*)	て **te** (*teh*)	と **to** (*toh*)
な **na** (*nah*)	に **ni** (*nee*)	ぬ **nu** (*noo*)	ね **ne** (*neh*)	の **no** (*noh*)
は **ha** (*hah*)	ひ **hi** (*hee*)	ふ **fu** (*foo*)	へ **he** (*heh*)	ほ **ho** (*hoh*)
ま **ma** (*mah*)	み **mi** (*mee*)	む **mu** (*moo*)	め **me** (*meh*)	も **mo** (*moh*)
や **ya** (*yah*)		ゆ **yu** (*yoo*)		よ **yo** (*yoh*)
ら **ra** (*rah*)	り **ri** (*ree*)	る **ru** (*roo*)	れ **re** (*reh*)	ろ **ro** (*roh*)
わ **wa** (*wah*)				を **o** (*oh*)

ん **n**				

が **ga** (*gah*)	ぎ **gi** (*gee*)	ぐ **gu** (*goo*)	げ **ge** (*geh*)	ご **go** (*goh*)
ざ **za** (*zah*)	じ **ji** (*jee*)	ず **zu** (*zoo*)	ぜ **ze** (*zeh*)	ぞ **zo** (*zoh*)
だ **da** (*dah*)	ぢ **ji** (*jee*)	づ **zu** (*zoo*)	で **de** (*deh*)	ど **do** (*doh*)
ば **ba** (*bah*)	び **bi** (*bee*)	ぶ **bu** (*boo*)	べ **be** (*beh*)	ぼ **bo** (*boh*)

ぱ **pa** (*pah*)	ぴ **pi** (*pee*)	ぷ **pu** (*poo*)	ぺ **pe** (*peh*)	ぽ **po** (*poh*)

きゃ **kya** (*kyah*)		きゅ **kyu** (*kyoo*)		きょ **kyo** (*kyoh*)
しゃ **sha** (*shah*)		しゅ **shu** (*shoo*)		しょ **sho** (*shoh*)
ちゃ **cha** (*chah*)		ちゅ **chu** (*choo*)		ちょ **cho** (*choh*)
にゃ **nya** (*nyah*)		にゅ **nyu** (*nyoo*)		にょ **nyo** (*nyoh*)
ひゃ **hya** (*hyah*)		ひゅ **hyu** (*hyoo*)		ひょ **hyo** (*hyoh*)
みゃ **mya** (*myah*)		みゅ **myu** (*myoo*)		みょ **myo** (*myoh*)
りゃ **rya** (*ryah*)		りゅ **ryu** (*ryoo*)		りょ **ryo** (*ryoh*)

ぎゃ **gya** (*gyah*)		ぎゅ **gyu** (*gyoo*)		ぎょ **gyo** (*gyoh*)
じゃ **ja** (*jah*)		じゅ **ju** (*joo*)		じょ **jo** (*joh*)
びゃ **bya** (*byah*)		びゅ **byu** (*byoo*)		びょ **byo** (*byoh*)
ぴゃ **pya** (*pyah*)		ぴゅ **pyu** (*pyoo*)		ぴょ **pyo** (*pyoh*)

KATAKANA

ア a (*ah*)	イ i (*ee*)	ウ u (*oo*)	エ e (*eh*)	オ o (*oh*)
カ ka (*kah*)	キ ki (*kee*)	ク ku (*koo*)	ケ ke (*keh*)	コ ko (*koh*)
サ sa (*sah*)	シ shi (*shee*)	ス su (*soo*)	セ se (*seh*)	ソ so (*soh*)
タ ta (*tah*)	チ chi (*chee*)	ツ tsu (*tsoo*)	テ te (*teh*)	ト to (*toh*)
ナ na (*nah*)	ニ ni (*nee*)	ヌ nu (*noo*)	ネ ne (*neh*)	ノ no (*noh*)
ハ ha (*hah*)	ヒ hi (*hee*)	フ fu (*foo*)	ヘ he (*heh*)	ホ ho (*hoh*)
マ ma (*mah*)	ミ mi (*mee*)	ム mu (*moo*)	メ me (*meh*)	モ mo (*moh*)
ヤ ya (*yah*)		ユ yu (*yoo*)		ヨ yo (*yoh*)
ラ ra (*rah*)	リ ri (*ree*)	ル ru (*roo*)	レ re (*reh*)	ロ ro (*roh*)
ワ wa (*wah*)				ヲ o (*oh*)

ン n				

ガ ga (*gah*)	ギ gi (*gee*)	グ gu (*goo*)	ゲ ge (*geh*)	ゴ go (*goh*)
ザ za (*zah*)	ジ ji (*jee*)	ズ zu (*zoo*)	ゼ ze (*zeh*)	ゾ zo (*zoh*)
ダ da (*dah*)	ヂ ji (*jee*)	ヅ zu (*zoo*)	デ de (*deh*)	ド do (*doh*)
バ ba (*bah*)	ビ bi (*bee*)	ブ bu (*boo*)	ベ be (*beh*)	ボ bo (*boh*)

パ pa (*pah*)	ピ pi (*pee*)	プ pu (*poo*)	ペ pe (*peh*)	ポ po (*poh*)
ファ fa (*fah*)	フィ fi (*fee*)	フ fu (*foo*)	フェ fe (*feh*)	フォ fo (*foh*)

キャ kya (*kyah*)		キュ kyu (*kyoo*)		キョ kyo (*kyoh*)
シャ sha (*shah*)		シュ shu (*shoo*)		ショ sho (*shoh*)
チャ cha (*chah*)		チュ chu (*choo*)		チョ cho (*choh*)
ニャ nya (*nyah*)		ニュ nyu (*nyoo*)		ニョ nyo (*nyoh*)
ヒャ hya (*hyah*)		ヒュ hyu (*hyoo*)		ヒョ hyo (*hyoh*)
ミャ mya (*myah*)		ミュ myu (*myoo*)		ミョ myo (*myoh*)
リャ rya (*ryah*)		リュ ryu (*ryoo*)		リョ ryo (*ryoh*)

ギャ gya (*gyah*)		ギュ gyu (*gyoo*)		ギョ gyo (*gyoh*)
ジャ ja (*jah*)		ジュ ju (*joo*)		ジョ jo (*joh*)
ビャ bya (*byah*)		ビュ byu (*byoo*)		ビョ byo (*byoh*)
ピャ pya (*pyah*)		ピュ pyu (*pyoo*)		ピョ pyo (*pyoh*)

COMMON SIGNS YOU'LL FIND IN JAPAN

Bank

Pharmacy

Public Phone

Post Office

Barber

Dentist

Police

美容室

Beauty Parlor

救急病院

Hospital with Emergency Room

tobu

1. tobimasu
2. tonde
3. tobimashita

aruku

1. arukimasu
2. aruite
3. arukimashita

miru

1. mimasu
2. mite
3. mimashita

dasu, okuru

1. dashimasu, okurimasu
2. dashite, okutte
3. dashimashita, okurimashita

kaeru, kōkan suru

1. kaemasu, kōkan shimasu
2. kaete, kōkan shite
3. kaemashita, kōkan shimashita

wakaru

1. wakarimasu
2. wakatte
3. wakarimashita

deru

1. demasu
2. dete
3. demashita

hoshii

1. hoshii desu
2. hoshii deshita

suwaru

1. suwarimasu
2. suwatte
3. suwarimashita

to fly

1. fly
2. flying
3. flew

to walk

1. walk
2. walking
3. walked

to see

1. see
2. seeing
3. saw

to send

1. send
2. sending
3. sent

to change, exchange

1. change, exchange
2. changing, exchanging
3. changed, exchanged

to understand

1. understand
2. understanding
3. understood

to depart

1. depart
2. departing
3. departed

to want

1. want
2. wanted

to sit, sit down

1. sit, sit down
2. sitting, sitting down
3. sat, sat down

uru

1. urimasu
2. utte
3. urimashita

shiru, shiriau

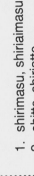
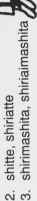

1. shirimasu, shiriaimasu
2. shitte, shiriatte
3. shirimashita, shiriaimashita

hanasu

1. hanashimasu
2. hanashite
3. hanashimashita

kiku

1. kikimasu
2. kiite
3. kikimashita

harau

1. haraimasu
2. haratte
3. haraimashita

ageru

1. agemasu
2. agete
3. agemashita

sagasu

1. sagashimasu
2. sagashite
3. sagashimashita

kau

1. kaimasu
2. katte
3. kaimashita

kaimono suru/shoppingu suru

1. kaimono shimasu/shoppingu shimasu
2. kaimono shite/shoppingu shite
3. kaimono shimashita/shoppingu shimashita

to sell

1. sell
2. selling
3. sold

to know, to get to know

1. know, get to know
2. knowing, getting to know
3. knew, got to know

to speak

1. speak
2. speaking
3. spoke

to ask

1. ask
2. asking
3. asked

to pay

1. pay
2. paying
3. paid

to give

1. give
2. giving
3. gave

to look for

1. look for
2. looking for
3. looked for

to buy

1. buy
2. buying
3. bought

to shop

1. shop
2. shopping
3. shopped

sain suru

1. sain shimasu
2. sain shite
3. sain shimashita

hakobu

1. hakobimasu
2. hakonde
3. hakobimashita

uketoru

1. uketorimasu
2. uketotte
3. uketorimashita

nemuru

1. nemurimasu
2. nemutte
3. nemurimashita

yorokobu, tanoshimu

1. yorokobimasu, tanoshimimasu
2. yorokonde, tanoshinde
3. yorokobimashita, tanoshimimashita

noru

1. norimasu
2. notte
3. norimashita

iu

1. iimasu
2. itte
3. iimashita

ireru

1. iremasu
2. irete
3. iremashita

dekiru

1. dekimasu
2. dekite
3. dekimashita

to sign

1. sign
2. signing
3. signed

to carry

1. carry
2. carrying
3. carried

to receive

1. receive
2. receiving
3. received

to sleep

1. sleep
2. sleeping
3. slept

to be pleased, to enjoy

1. be pleased, enjoy
2. being pleased, enjoying
3. was (were) pleased, enjoyed

to get on, ride on

1. get on, ride on
2. getting on, riding on
3. got on, rode on

to say, tell

1. say, tell
2. saying, telling
3. said, told

to put in

1. put in
2. putting in
3. put in

to be able, can

1. be able, can
2. being able, can
3. was (were) able, could

samui

ii, oishii

hidari

takai

warui, yoku nai

subarashii, kirei, ii

ōkii

atsui

totemo

cold	good, delicious	left
expensive	bad, wrong	wonderful, beautiful, nice, good
large, big	hot	very, a lot

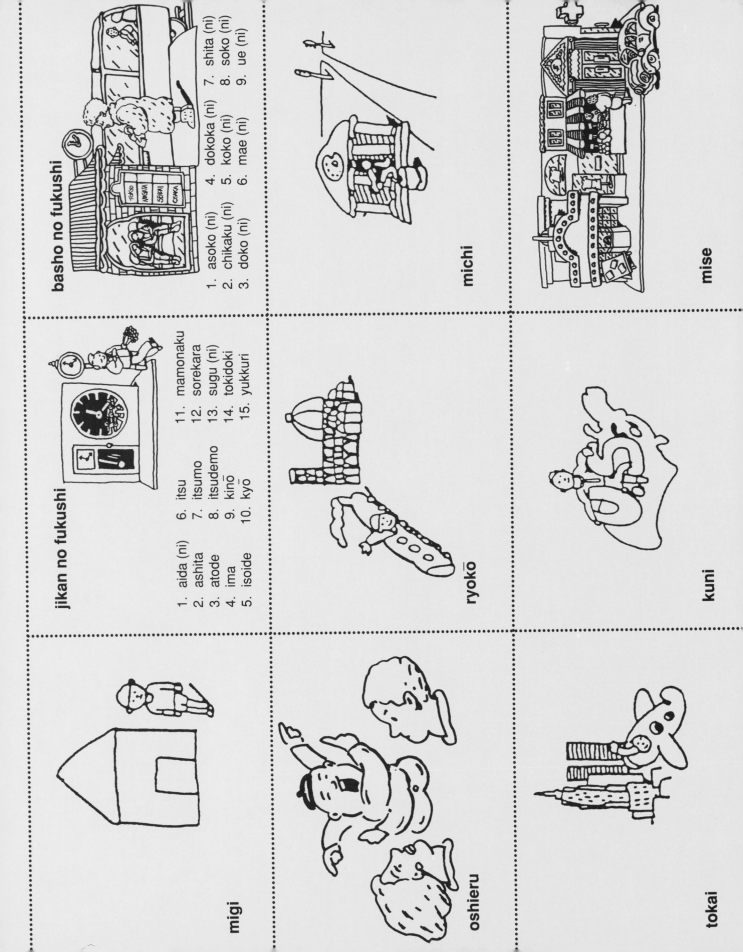

basho no fukushi

1. asoko (ni)
2. chikaku (ni)
3. doko (ni)
4. dokoka (ni)
5. koko (ni)
6. mae (ni)
7. shita (ni)
8. soko (ni)
9. ue (ni)

michi

mise

jikan no fukushi

1. aida (ni)
2. ashita
3. atode
4. ima
5. isoide
6. itsu
7. itsumo
8. itsudemo
9. kinō
10. kyō
11. mamonaku
12. sorekara
13. sugu (ni)
14. tokidoki
15. yukkuri

ryokō

kuni

migi

oshieru

tokai

adverbs of place

1. over there
2. near, nearby
3. where
4. somewhere
5. here
6. before, in front of
7. under, below
8. there
9. above, on, up

adverbs of time

1. while
2. tomorrow
3. after, later
4. now
5. quickly
6. when
7. always
8. any time
9. yesterday
10. today
11. soon
12. then
13. immediately
14. sometimes
15. slowly

right

street, road, way

trip

to tell, teach, explain

shop, store

country

city

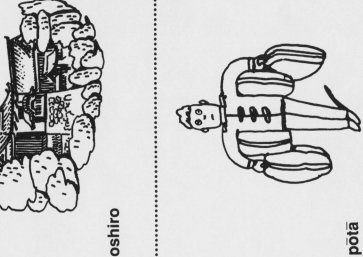

ginkō

oshiro

pōtā

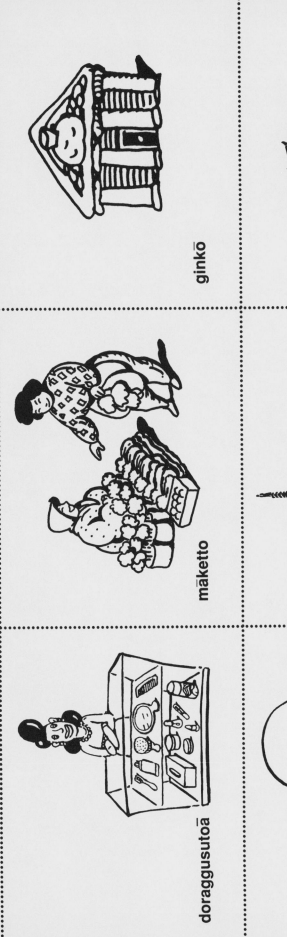

māketto

otera

kisha

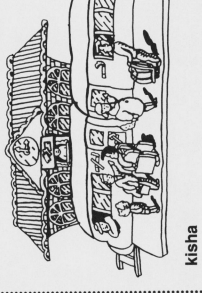

doraggusutoā

hoteru

ken, kippu

bank

castle

porter

market

temple

train

drugstore

hotel

ticket

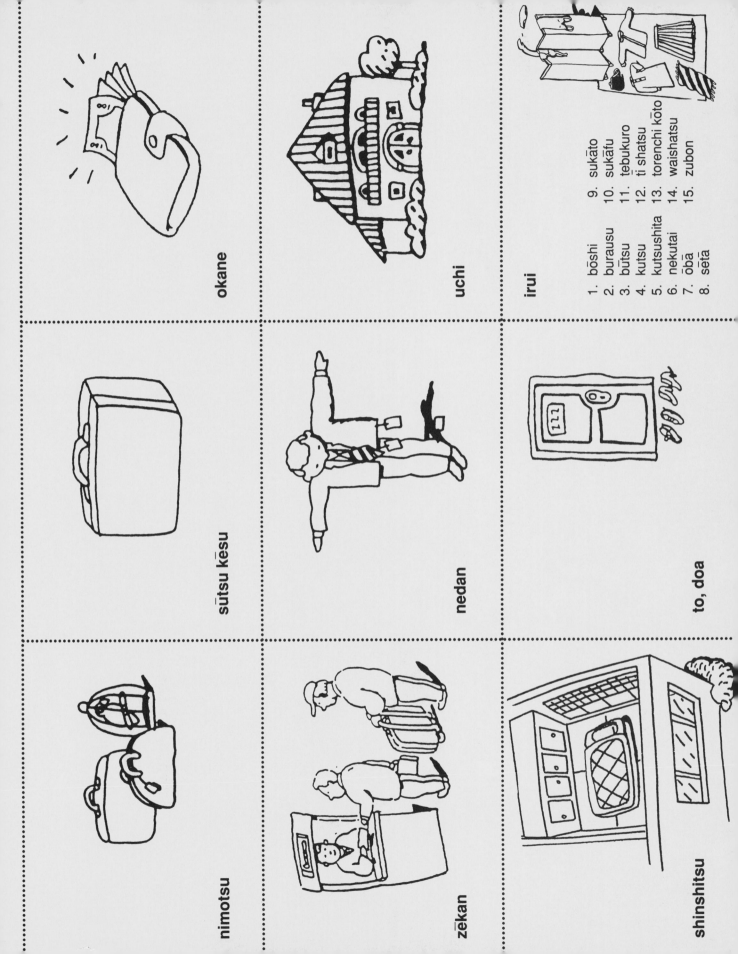

okane

uchi

irui

1.	bōshi	9.	sukāto
2.	burausu	10.	sukāfu
3.	būtsu	11.	tebukuro
4.	kutsu	12.	ti shatsu
5.	kutsushita	13.	torenchi kōto
6.	nekutai	14.	waishatsu
7.	ōbā	15.	zubon
8.	sētā		

sūtsu kēsu

nedan

to, doa

nimotsu

zēkan

shinshitsu

money

house

suitcase

price

door

baggage, luggage

customs

bedroom

clothing, outfit

1. cap, hat
2. blouse
3. boot
4. shoe
5. sock

6. tie
7. overcoat
8. sweater
9. skirt
10. scarf

11. glove
12. tee shirt
13. trench coat
14. shirt
15. pants, trousers

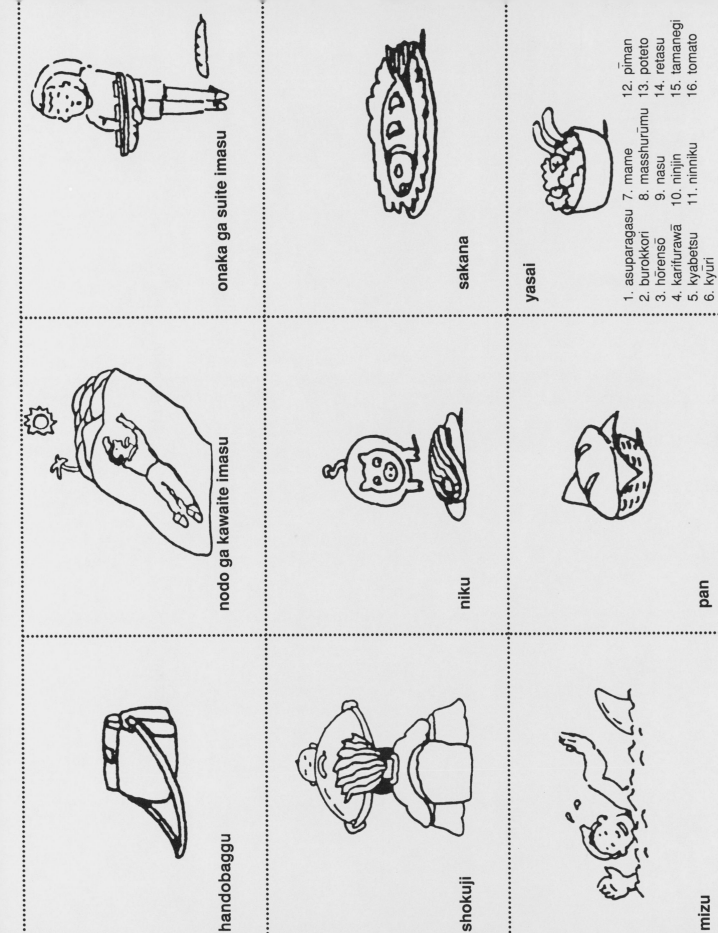

onaka ga suite imasu

sakana

yasai

1. asuparagasu
2. burokkori
3. hōrensō
4. karifurawā
5. kyabetsu
6. kyūri
7. mame
8. masshurūmu
9. nasu
10. ninjin
11. ninniku
12. pīman
13. poteto
14. retasu
15. tamanegi
16. tomato

nodo ga kawaite imasu

niku

pan

handobaggu

shokuji

mizu

to be hungry

to be thirsty

purse

fish

meat

meal

vegetables

1. asparagus
2. broccoli
3. spinach
4. cauliflower
5. cabbage
6. cucumber
7. peas, beans
8. mushroom
9. eggplant
10. carrot
11. garlic
12. green pepper
13. potato
14. lettuce
15. onion
16. tomato

bread

water

shokki

1. fōku
2. kōhii jawan
3. koppu
4. naifu
5. napukin
6. osara
7. supūn
8. wain gurasu

tsuki

1. ichi gatsu
2. ni gatsu
3. san gatsu
4. shi gatsu
5. go gatsu
6. roku gatsu
7. shichi gatsu
8. hachi gatsu
9. ku gatsu
10. jū gatsu
11. jūichi gatsu
12. jūni gatsu

kisetsu

1. fuyu
2. haru
3. natsu
4. aki

tabemono

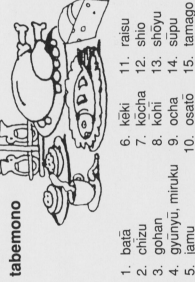

1. batā
2. chīzu
3. gohan
4. gyūnyū, miruku
5. jamu
6. kēki
7. kōcha
8. kōhi
9. ocha
10. osatō
11. raisu
12. shio
13. shōyu
14. sūpu
15. tamago

hi

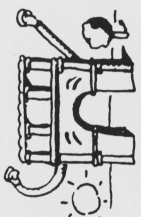

1. asa
2. gogo
3. gozen
4. hiru
5. hiruma
6. yoru
7. yūgata

tenki

1. ame
2. arashi
3. atsui
4. hare
5. kion
6. kumori
7. mushiatsui
8. samui
9. suzushii
10. yuki

kudamono

1. banana
2. budō
3. gurēpufurūtsu
4. ichigo
5. ichijiku
6. meron
7. mikan
8. momo
9. nashi
10. orenji
11. painappuru
12. puramu/sumomo
13. ringo
14. sakuranbo/cherī
15. yō nashi

yōbi

1. getsu yōbi
2. ka yōbi
3. sui yōbi
4. moku yōbi
5. kin yōbi
6. do yōbi
7. nichi yōbi

jikan

1. fun/pun
2. han
3. ji
4. ~ji
5. mezamashi
6. tokei

tableware

1. fork
2. coffee cup
3. cup
4. knife
5. napkin
6. plate
7. spoon
8. wine glass

months

1. January
2. February
3. March
4. April
5. May
6. June
7. July
8. August
9. September
10. October
11. November
12. December

seasons

1. winter
2. spring
3. summer
4. fall

foods

1. butter
2. cheese
3. rice (cooked)
4. milk
5. jam
6. cake
7. tea (western)
8. coffee
9. tea (Japanese)
10. sugar
11. rice (on plate)
12. salt
13. soy sauce
14. soup
15. egg

time of day

1. morning
2. P.M., afternoon
3. A.M., in the morning
4. noon
5. daytime
6. night
7. dusk, early evening

weather

1. rain
2. storm
3. hot
4. fine
5. temperature
6. overcast
7. hot and humid
8. cold
9. cool
10. snow

fruits

1. banana
2. grapes
3. grapefruit
4. strawberries
5. fig
6. melon
7. tangerine
8. peach
9. Japanese pear
10. orange
11. pineapple
12. plum
13. apple
14. cherries
15. pear

days of the week

1. Monday
2. Tuesday
3. Wednesday
4. Thursday
5. Friday
6. Saturday
7. Sunday

time

1. minute
2. half (past)
3. hour
4. o'clock
5. alarm clock
6. watch, clock

san

te

iro

1. aka
2. ao, kon
3. kiiro
4. kuro
5. midori
6. shiro

---

kazoku (2)

1. chichi, otōsan
2. haha, okāsan
3. kodomo, okosan
4. musuko, musuko san
5. musume, ojōsan
6. otto, goshujin
7. tsuma, okusan

akachan

karada

1. ashi
2. atama
3. ha
4. hiji
5. hiza
6. kata
7. kubi
8. kuchi
9. me
10. mimi
11. mune
12. onaka
13. oshiri
14. senaka
15. shita
16. te
17. ude
18. yubi

---

kazoku (1)

1. chichi, otōsan
2. haha, okāsan
3. mago, omago san
4. oba, obasan
5. oji, ojisan
6. sobo, obāsan
7. sofu, ojiisan

tomodachi

atama

Mr., Mrs., Ms., Miss.

hand

family (2)

1. father
2. mother
3. child
4. son
5. daughter
6. husband
7. wife

colors

1. red
2. blue
3. yellow
4. black
5. green
6. white

body

1. leg
2. head
3. tooth
4. elbow
5. knee
6. shoulder
7. neck
8. mouth
9. eye
10. ear
11. chest
12. stomach (belly)
13. hip (fanny)
14. back
15. tongue
16. hand
17. arm
18. finger

baby

family (1)

1. father
2. mother
3. grandchild
4. aunt
5. uncle
6. grandmother
7. grandfather

head

friend